D0130446

Reprint 2000
First English edition 1996
First published in German 1993

Copyright © original German text:
Rainer Horbelt and Sonja Spindler
Copyright © English edition: Vista Ibérica Publicações

Published in English by Vista Ibérica Publicações, Lda
N.I.P.C. 504 788 671

Address:     Urb. Lagoa Sol, Lote 1 - B
             8400-415 Lagoa - Algarve - Portugal
             Tel.: +351 282 340 660
             Fax: +351 282 343 088
             E-mail: vistaiberica@mail.telepac.pt

Printed by  Empresa Litográfica do Sul, S.A.
            8901 Vila Real Santo António

Depósito Legal: 105030/96
ISBN 972-8044-20-8

# Algarve Country Cooking

Rainer Horbelt

◆

Sonja Spindler

English translation by Jutta Zieren-Drew

## VISTA IBÉRICA

by agreement with the Foto-Museum Buchverlags, Herne

# CONTENTS

## AUTUMN · 95

## WINTER · 139

# PREFACE

A cookery book? Another one? Surely there are enough cookery books on the market? And a cookery book about dishes in the Algarve?

Many people may doubt there is anything like a distinctive cuisine here. We think there is and we believe it is of special interest. That's why we decided to write this book. But before talking about cooking, a few thoughts on the place and its people.

The south coast of the Algarve, Portugal's most southerly province, runs for about 150 kilometres from Vila Real de St. António on the Spanish border, to Sagres which is the most extreme south-westerly corner of Europe. The hinterland is fertile with an abundance of vineyards and orchards. Then there are the hills, the *serras*, which for hundreds of years have helped to keep the rest of Europe at bay.

For most Portuguese, those living in the middle and the north of the country, the Algarve could almost be Africa. They have difficulties understanding the Algarvians - and that does not just refer to their spoken language.

The Algarvians are as Portuguese as the Welsh or Scots are British. A gentle people, formerly farmers and fishermen, they are now experiencing the effects of tourism on their native environment. As they profit from this change with improved living conditions, they accept they may lose some of their traditions. This is one of the reasons why we have written this book.

We hope that regional culinary traditions and customs will not be forgotten, that little-known local delicacies will be recorded before those who can prepare them are gone forever, and that a few of the recipes on the pages that follow become more widely appreciated. We hope also that some form of contemporary history is being gathered and preserved before hamburgers and the like take over any further.

With this in mind we went exploring the kitchens of the Algarve. We would like to take you along on a similar expedition. What is there to discover? We think we can show you some totally new dishes as well as a few ways of preparing food that may strike you as unusual.

Algarvians go in for wholesome, unadulterated, native cooking. The dishes eaten bv fishermen and farmers are prepared from ingredients which come straight from the land and the sea. Left-overs are used up in a variety of stews. They have ways of preparing food which have held good for many generations. More recently the long and close association with Portugal's former colonies in distant parts of the world has also played a significant part in influencing the food of the Algarve.

Fish and pork are the predominant ingredients in the diet of farming and fishing families, along with olives, figs, broad beans and cabbage. Fish in the Algarve is nearly always fresh, of course. Even visitors who are normally quite spoilt when it comes to food may be pleasantly surprised by the variety of fish available and the imaginative ways it is prepared.

Of the meats, the Algarvians eat pork, mutton, lamb, goat and lots of poultry. Beef is not traditional, but is now available everywhere. Game - mostly rabbit, but also wild boar from the mountains - is sometimes on offer. There are quite a few dishes with offal.

Generally one eats less meat here than in Britain or Germany, for example. Considering this is a southern European country, the quality of the meat is remarkably good, though the way the butchers here cut their meat may seem rather strange to northern Europeans.

The home-made sausages of the Algarve, whether smoked or air-dried, are a delicacy. They are an inseparable part of very many recipes. The Algarvians use them to add spice to their dishes. The ham from Monchique is an experience. Should you order a *melão com presunto* (melon and ham) in a restaurant, you can be reasonably sure that the ingredients originate in the region, maybe from the farm next door. Fresh sausages, on the other hand, are a catastrophe. Most are a poor imitation of imported products. The Algarvians don't eat them.

Fresh vegetables and fruit are available throughout the year - that is to say local fruit and vegetables, not the imported kind. Again, one is impressed by the variety on offer in the markets. Special mention should be made of *nêsperas*, a yellow fruit which mystifies many visitors from northern Europe. Native to the Far East, *nêsperas* are plentiful in the Algarve in early summer and are known in English as loquats. Then there is *xu-xu*, a vegetable which tastes like kohlrabi cabbage, only more delicate.

In the Algarve, fruit and vegetables are unusually fresh. That is because their journey to the consumer is so short and because farmers themselves sell directly to the market. Here you buy and sell produce because it tastes good not because it corresponds with EU regulations or merely looks nice. Strictly seasonal, the various kinds of fresh fruit and vegetables appear in Algarve markets as soon they are ripe in the fields. They disappear just as suddenly.

Locally-produced cheese is disappointing, perhaps with the exception of the sheep or goat's cheese that the shepherds themselves bring to the required level of maturity at home. One can buy a large assortment of other Portuguese or imported cheeses in the Algarve, but they are not always cheap. Roughly speaking, one can distinguish four different types of Portuguese cheese: *Ilha* from the Azores; *Serra* made from cow's and goat's milk; *Queijo Marofa*, similar to Edam; and a tasty equivalent to Camembert.

The Algarvians use herbs such as *coentros*, green coriander leaves, previously unknown to us. And they often use familiar herbs in unfamiliar ways. Cinnamon with meat, for example. Can you imagine this? Wait and see.

There are not that many dough mixtures - too few for our liking - but they are used for all shapes and sizes of loaves and bread rolls.

The Algarvians have a passion for sweets and at times their sweets are terribly sweet. They make them with masses of eggs, sugar (often available here as unrefined, brown sugar), little butter and still less cream. They also use some specially prepared ingredients such as *fios de ovos*, *ovos moles*, *doce de chila* and their special marzipan, all products that are unique and well worth discovering.

As for other products: free-range eggs can be bought in

every market; rice produced in the US is helping to make local paddy-fields redundant; the quality of the local wine is such that we prefer here to point to the chapter in which we have written about it, but the local spirits are highly recommended. Milk and cream are relatively expensive and are barely used in cooking. Maybe this is one of the reasons why there are so few sauces.

Tourism has had some positive effects. A few traditional kitchen devices, like the *cataplana*, have been rediscovered because they sell well as souvenirs.

What else have we noticed? Well, the prices. They have greatly increased in recent years. There was a time when all types of food and drink produced in Portugal could be bought in the Algarve at unexpectedly low prices. That is no longer true. Many items are now as expensive as in the United Kingdom and North America. Some are more so.

Eating out is still relatively cheap, though beware of establishments which take advantage of tourists. Restaurants or cafes frequented by the local community and run by people who know their job often give better value than one would get back home.

At first glance, Algarvian dishes seem relatively straightforward to prepare, but after listening to intricate explanations from local cooks and working through their long, handwritten instruction notes, everything seemed to become much more complicated. We have taken the liberty of simplifying a few matters.

This is going to be a book for people who either spend their holidays in the Algarve or live here permanently. We hope it will help you to get to know the specialities of the region and encourage you to cook one or two of the dishes yourself. We have modified some of the recipes, without changing their essence, so that they may be tried out at home.

Have we aroused your curiosity? If so, please join us on our journey through the Algarve seasons.....

Spring

Spring in the Algarve arrives with the orange blossom. The air is impregnated with its incomparable scent.

A carpet of flowers, both wild and planted, covers the unfinished and incomplete made visible by winter. Their colourful blossoms conceal the scars that "civilisation" has cut into the ground.

The Algarvians greet the spring with a bouquet of blades of wheat, branches from pomegranate and olive trees, sometimes poppies and brambles, which they tie to their front doors.

Spring attracts the first tourist crowds of the year. The visitors arrive by air or by car, hungry for the sun and for adventure. The Algarvians make space for them. Their houses have been freshly painted, their fields are ploughed and they have time to relax. They look kindly and with a certain air of composure upon those who glance into their gardens or merely pass by.

We asked four different restaurants to present menus that represented each of the seasons of the year and to reveal the secrets of their preparation. Quite intentionally we chose four very different restaurants, all highly recommended. This does not mean, of course, that there are not many other highly recommendable restaurants.

Before we introduce the first restaurant, something in general needs to be said about restaurants in the Algarve. They are a great many of them and competition for business is fierce. This is bad for the restaurant owners, good for the customers.

The Algarve's multi-cultural society provides restaurants with international cuisine plus a large variety of national menus - Chinese, Angolan, Indian, Vietnamese, German and so on. There are not too many typically Portuguese or Algarvian dishes, although most restaurants do have at least a few to choose from.

There are four classifications for restaurants, from third (*terceira*) up to luxury class (*de luxo*). Most restaurants display their classification right by the entrance door. This classification refers to the standard of the premises, not the quality of the food or the service.

A menu, sometimes written in several languages, is

displayed outside every restaurant. Inside, there should be another display or menu of all listed dishes, drinks and their prices. The price of the soups and possibly a glance at what is emerging from the kitchen will give an indication of price and quality.

If you go to a restaurant frequented by local residents and run by people who know their job, you usually find that you spend less (for better quality) than you would back at home.

Restaurants are obliged to offer a *menu de turista*, a "tourist menu," which is particularly reasonable in price. It is worth checking if a restaurant offers a *prato do dia*, "dish of the day." This is usually quite a cheap meal and a very fresh one.

Some dishes on the menu may have a variable price. This is indicated as P.V. (*preço variável*). It usually applies to the most expensive types of seafood, priced per kilo.

All restaurant prices usually include VAT. (IVA in Portugal) and service charges. If you are pleased with the service, a 10% tip on top of the cost of the meal will be appreciated.

Menus should also include the price and description of the cover (bread, butter, maybe fresh cheese, olives etc.). In most cases a cover will be served automatically, but if you do not want it, you may send it back and you will not be charged for it.

Meal times coincide roughly with those in other European countries. Dinner, the main meal of the day, is served from 6.0pm or 7.00 pm, until about 9.30 pm, or later in summer.

Should there be a reason to complain about the meal or the service, ask for the manager, *o gerente* or *o patrão*. If that is to no avail, you can ask for the official complaints' book (*o livro das reclamações*) which the authorities are supposed to review when renewing licences.

By the way, to call the waiter in a restaurant can be quite difficult. There is no appropriate form of address. If you can't catch his eye, it is best to hail him with an "excuse me" or, better still, *"faz favor."*

# A SPRING MENU
# FROM ADEGA VILA LISA
# IN MEXILHOEIRA GRANDE

Adega Vila Lisa is to be found right in the centre of the village of Mexilhoeira Grande between Lagos and Portimão. There are no signboards and no advertising to indicate that this tiny house is actually a restaurant. Only the local residents know about it.

The owner, José Duarte Silva, was born in Mexilhoeira Grande. The name of the *adega* is an anagram of his surname.

José has never trained as a chef. He is an artist, a painter. For many years he lived in Lisbon and he has had exhibitions in many major towns in Portugal. His paintings are also displayed on the walls of the *adega*. A few years ago he returned to his home villahe to work as a painter. Cooking is his passion and the restaurant is his hobby.

It all started as a meal for friends, as a joke really. It was a single one-course meal. José is still cooking it to this day. It is called *Rabo de boi com grão*.

## OXTAIL AND CHICK PEAS *RABO DE BOI COM GRÃO*

| | |
|---|---|
| *1 kilo oxtail* | *500 g chick peas* |
| *3 garlic cloves* | *1 tbsp pork lard* |
| *250 ml red wine* | *250 g pumpkin* |
| *salt, pepper* | *2 tomatoes* |
| *laurel leaf* | *1 cup celery leaves* |
| *2 onions* | *finely chopped* |
| *3 cloves* | |

Soak the chick peas overnight and cook in 1 litre of water until soft.

Lightly fry pieces of oxtail in hot oil.

Cut pumpkin, tomatoes and onions into cubes; finely chop garlic and add to the oxtail.

Add spices to red wine and pour over oxtail. Cover and let simmer. Add a little water as necessary.

When the meat starts to separate from the bone, add the chick peas. Simmer over a low heat for another 10 minutes.

Serve on a hot plate.

Garnish with celery leaves.

If you visit Adega Vila Lisa you will forget everything you normally expect or demand from a normal restaurant.

There are no menus. You will be offered what José himself has bought fresh in the market and prepared for the day.

The way it works is this: Every guest receives the same meal, three or four courses, sometimes more, at a very reasonable fixed price, drinks inclusive.

There is no advertising and there are no fixed opening or closing times. In spring, autumn and winter, José opens only on Friday and Saturday nights (if he hasn't decided to close, that is). During the summer months of July, August and September, he is open every night.

It is advisable to phone to make sure a table is available. The restaurant is tiny and although José says he can seat 40 inside, well ....

During the summer months more seats are available in the garden, which makes it possible for 150 meals to be served from the tiny kitchen. His clientele is made up of artists and tourists, local residents and personal friends, sometimes prominent local politicians. It is a colourful mixture. Because tables and benches are long and close, one easily establishes contact with other diners. This may not be to everyone's liking, but if expectations are not set too high one can have a lot of fun.

Here is José Duarte Silva's spring menu: *Raia de alhada* for starters, *Favas Algarvias* as the main course, *Queijo de figo* as dessert.

## SKATE SALAD *RAIA DE ALHADA*

| | |
|---|---|
| *1 skate (or other flatfish)* | *2 tbsp vinegar* |
| *6 garlic cloves* | *salt, pepper* |
| *1/2 cup olive oil* | |

Clean the skate and cook in salt water with a little bit of garlic until tender.

Take off the skin and tear the meat into small pieces. Prepare a sauce using vinegar, oil and the remaining garlic crushed in its skin. Add one part of oil to three parts of fish stock.

Mix fish and sauce just like a salad, add salt and pepper. Serve with French bread.

*Favas,* the main ingredient of the main course, are broad beans. *Favas* and *ervilhas* (green peas), vegetables of the Algarve since time immemorial, are sown in early winter and hence always fresh in winter and spring.

## BROAD BEANS ALGARVE-STYLE *FAVAS ALGARVIAS*

| | |
|---|---|
| *1 kilo broad beans* | *1 tsp fresh garlic leaves* |
| *1 tsp fresh green coriander leaves* | *1 tbsp fresh celery leaves* |
| | *1 tbsp olive oil* |
| *1 cup onion rings* | *200 g chouriço* |
| *200 g lean bacon* | *1 chopped garlic clove* |
| *2 cups beef stock* | *salt* |

Cook the beans in stock or salt water until soft. Drain. Sauté garlic in olive oil, add herbs and mix with beans.

Cut bacon and sausages into slices, add onions and fry in saucepan. Pour over beans.

José serves the *favas* with grilled sardines and green lettuce. Fried or boiled potatoes would be just as nice.

The recipe mentions *chouriço* as an ingredient. This is a sausage and page 100 describes how it is made.

There are no desserts in the traditional sense in Vila Lisa. At the end of a meal José serves his home-made speciality: Fig cheese. It is so called because it looks like a cheese, but it is a sweet, a very special one.

A strong coffee (a *bica* or *espresso*) will then be served and along with it, most importantly, a *medronho*, a spirit made from the berries of the arbutus or strawberry tree.

## FIG CHEESE *QUEIJO DE FIGO*

| | |
|---|---|
| *250 g figs* | *250 g almonds* |
| *100 g sugar* | *a small glass of medronho* |
| *1 tsp aniseed* | *1 tbsp ground lemon peel* |
| *sugar to garnish* | |

Mince the figs with a meat grinder.
Chop almonds into fine and rough bits.

Mix all ingredients and cook in a saucepan on a low heat until sticky. Cool down and then shape into small balls, press flat and roll in sugar.

The preparation of *Queijo de Maio* is similar except that the pieces are slightly larger and shaped like bread.

## FIG CAKE *QUEIJO DE MAIO*

| | |
|---|---|
| *1 kilo figs* | *1 kilo almonds* |
| *1 tbsp cinnamon* | *2 tbsp aniseed* |
| *500 g sugar* | *200 g cocoa* |
| *two ground lemon peels* | *1 egg white* |
| *1 glass aguardente* | *whole almonds for decoration* |
| *icing sugar* | *lemon juice for the icing* |

The preparation is the same as for Vila Lisa's Fig cheese.

Put the dry figs and part of the almonds through the meat grinder. Roughly chop remaining almonds. According to taste, you may skin the almonds and roast in the oven before chopping.

Beat the egg white in a large bowl and mix all ingredients to a dough. Shape into a round or long loaf. Wrap into wax paper and leave in refrigerator for a few days before eating.

The cake can be covered with icing and decorated with whole almonds and dried figs.

The literal translation of *Queijo de Maio*, is "May cheese". The name is derived from the fact that Portuguese families traditionally eat it on the first of May, a national holiday.

# FIOS DE OVOS,
# OVOS MOLES
# AND
# DOCE DE CHILA

Before we introduce you to Algarvian sweet recipes we have
to show you a few essential ways of dealing with the main ingredients, *fios de ovos, ovos moles* and *doce de chila*.

These barely translatable concoctions are used as fillings,
decoration or side-dishes to many cakes and sweets. The pastry
and cake-shops in the Algarve could not do without them.

It has to be said here that these specialities are easy to make
yet so cleverly used. They could assume an interesting role in
patisseries elsewhere.

First of all those spaghetti-like strips of egg called *fios de ovos* which are a very old and traditional Portuguese speciality. Their description is to be found in every Portuguese cookery book. Every region has its own way of making *fios*.

## FIOS DE OVOS

| | |
|---|---|
| *20 egg yolks* | *1 whole egg* |
| *1 l water* | *750 g sugar* |
| *1 l cold sugar water appr.* | |

Separate the yolks from the whites in a sieve. Do not stir but make marks with a knife to and fro until the yolks are of thin consistency in a basin underneath. Do likewise with the whole egg. Boil vigorously in a medium-sized pot on high heat 1 litre of water with the sugar until the sugar water pearls slowly from a spoon. Lower the flame.

Take a special funnel (*funil de fios de ovos*) and let the yolk run with circular movements into the sugar syrup. Hold the funnel as high as possible in order to make the egg threads as thin as possible. Do a little quantity at a time.

Lift the *fios de ovos* with a straining ladle and dip them into the cold sugar water. Continue until the yolks are finished. Take the *fios de ovos* up with a fork and dry them on a cloth.

The recipe mentions a *funil de fios de ovos*, which you can buy in a Portuguese household shop or at a market. It is a funnel with several small holes.

The quality of the *fios de ovos* depends on the quality of the eggs. *Fios de ovos* are used for filings as well as decoration of cakes and sweets. They can also be an edible part of a table decoration.

They can be kept in the fridge for up to a week, or frozen for longer.

Another speciality of the sweet Portuguese cuisine are *ovos moles*, a kind of egg custard usually used as fillings in cakes and sweets.

| OVOS MOLES | |
| --- | --- |
| *10 egg yolks* | *250 g sugar* |
| *1/2 litre water* | *1 tsp cornflour* |

Bring sugar and water to the boil. Dissolve cornflour in a little water and mix with sugared water. Take the saucepan off the heat.

Pass the egg yolks through a fine sieve into the syrup. Gently stir until you have a creamy texture.

You may add lemon, or orange peel, or even orange juice to the cream.

By adding ground almonds to this mixture its name changes to *rebuçado de ovos*.

*Ovos moles* can be used with food colouring.

For the last of our very basic recipes we need to take a special pumpkin, a *chila*. Outside Portugal it is not easy to find but, as a substitute, one could use an ordinary pumpkin. We have tried it with ordinary pumpkin strings and although the result was not perfect, it was quite acceptable.

## PUMPKIN JAM *DOCE DE CHILA*

| *1 chila* | *1/2 litre water* |
|---|---|
| *500 g sugar* | |

Place the *chila* pumpkin on your kitchen table. Take a heavy object (i.e. a saucepan) and hit it hard to break it open.

Take a wooden spoon and gently scoop out the white strings (and only those). Avoid under all circumstances taking either the black seeds or the yellow strands (called *tripas*, meaning innards) that are attached to the white ones.

Wash the pumpkin strings several times in a sieve in running water. Lay out on a piece of cloth and dry with gentle touches.

In an enamel saucepan bring water and sugar to the boil until the liquid is reduced by half and just about to thicken.

Add the pumpkin strings and continue to cook until the liquid is almost gone, then drain.

The above is a shortened version of the elaborate way the Algarvians go about making *doce de chila*. The Algarvians consider its preparation a science. They insist that the pumpkin must not be smashed with a heavy object, but dropped onto the floor to break open of its own accord. There are strict rules about not using any metal instrument to scoop out the strings, or even a knife to cut the pumpkin. Cooking time is very long and the strings will have to be washed again and again. We decided to shorten the preparation time so as not to spoil your fun.

*Doce de chila* is used as a filling. The strings deep-freeze easily. A variation of appearance and taste can be achieved by adding colour, cinnamon, vanilla, orange peel or anything similar to the syrup.

If you are not feeling adventurous enough to make it yourself, here's a tip: you can buy *doce de chila* ready-made in most supermarkets (on the shelf with the marmalade).

# SPRING RECIPES

Most of the local people in the Algarve have retained a bond to the countryside in which they live and to the change of seasons that go with it.

They eat fish when it tastes best. They collect their fruit and turn it into the most amazing produce only when it is ripe on the trees and shrubs. They buy their vegetables when they are harvested.

Asparagus is imported from somewhere in the southern hemisphere in winter but it is not often found in the markets. The Algarvians, using a lot of imagination, prefer to stick to their own regional produce.

Harvest time coincides with sowing time in more northerly

places. That is the case throughout the year practically.

In presenting the following recipes, we have made the adjustment to the cycle of seasons in southern Portugal. Most importantly, we are going to deal only with what is being harvested and what the Algarvians themselves cook and eat in springtime - fresh vegetables mostly.

## PEA SOUP *SOPA DE ERVILHAS*

| | |
|---|---|
| 2 cups fresh green peas | 1 onion, chopped |
| 3/4 litre beef stock | 1 tbsp oil |
| salt, pepper to season | 1 cup roasted bread cubes |

Heat the oil in a saucepan and sauté the onion until golden brown. Add the peas, stir and add the stock.

Cook until very tender.

Pass through a sieve, add salt and pepper to taste, sprinkle on roasted bread cubes.

## BROAD BEAN SOUP *SOPA DE FAVAS*

| | |
|---|---|
| 500 g broad beans | 1 carrot |
| 1 large onion | 100 g smoked ham or sausage |
| 1 cup of boiled rice | 1 1/2 litre vegetable stock |
| salt, pepper to season | 2 tbsp oil |

Heat the oil in a saucepan, add finely chopped onion and carrot, and allow to get brown.

Add stock, then add broad beans and cook until tender.

Add ham or sausage cubes and the rice. Season with salt and pepper.

(Back home you might wish to add savory, but this is hardly known in the Algarve).

## PRATO DAS CENOURAS

| | |
|---|---|
| *500 g carrots* | *250 g peas* |
| *500 g potatoes* | *1 tsp butter* |
| *8 eggs* | *1/2 tsp dill* |
| *salt, pepper to season* | *1 tbsp parsley* |
| *1 cup water* | |

Clean the carrots. Peel potatoes, wash and cut both into small cubes.

Heat the butter in a saucepan and add carrots, potatoes and peas. Stir and cook for two minutes. Add water.

Add salt, pepper and dill to taste. Cover and simmer until tender.

Chop parsley and sprinkle on vegetables. Serve with two fried eggs per person.

## Fish Pancakes *BOLINHOS DE PEIXE*

| | |
|---|---|
| *500 g fish fillet* | *1 egg* |
| *1 onion* | *1 tbsp parsley* |
| *3 tbsp breadcrumbs* | *salt, pepper* |

Mince or mix fish, parsley and onion in a blender. Make into a dough together with egg and breadcrumbs. Finely season with salt and pepper.

Form hand-size cakes. Fry in a frying-pan in hot oil until golden.

## Tongue with Rice and Peas *ARROZ DE LÍNGUA*

| | |
|---|---|
| *1 calf tongue* | *2 pigs' tongues* |
| *1 l water* | *half a laurel leaf* |
| *2 cups boiled rice* | *2 cups shelled peas* |
| *1 leek finely chopped* | *1 tsp flour* |
| *1/2 cup white wine* | *1 tblsp oil* |
| *salt, pepper* | |

Wash the tongues. Put into 1 litre of boiling salt water with the laurel. Boil until tender. Take out of the broth, skin and clean. Cut into thin stripes.

Heat the oil in a pot. Add leek and peas, but do not burn. Sprinkle with flour, add the wine and half a cup of the cooking broth. Season with salt and pepper. Let boil 5 to 10 min. Mix rice, tongue and vegetables and serve.

## NINHOS (A DESSERT WITH *DOCE DE CHILA*)

| | |
|---|---|
| *4 cups of doce de chila* | *4 egg yolk* |
| *4 tbsp sugar* | *1 tsp cinnamon* |
| *1 tbsp double cream* | |

Make little nests of *doce de chila* in glass dishes.

In a bain-marie mix egg yolk, cinnamon, cream and sugar and pour into the nests.

Red wine, cocoa or Mocha can be added according to taste. Allow to cool.

In the Algarve and the rest of Portugal there are many different ways of preparing *filhós*, those little cakes cooked in hot oil that are on offer everywhere in the markets.

Here is a recipe from Maria do Carmo in Algoz. It is regarded as something really special.

## FILHÓS

| | |
|---|---|
| *40 g yeast, 1 kg flour* | *1 tbsp ground lemon peel* |
| *1 tbsp ground orange peel* | *1 tsp aniseed* |
| *1 cup water* | *cinnamon and sugar to garnish* |
| *a pinch of salt* | *1 cup sugar* |
| *2 eggs, oil* | *1 cup milk* |

Pour one cup of boiling water over lemon, orange peel and aniseed and stand for 10 minutes. Pour through a sieve.

Mix the still warm liquid with flour and yeast and allow to rise.

Mix with flour, eggs, a pinch of salt and kneed into dough. Add some milk to make it more workable. Cover and stand for at least one hour.

Form little balls and allow to stand again.

Heat the oil.

Flatten the balls and fry in hot oil until golden brown.

Sprinkle with cinnamon and sugar.

(Instead of water, one can use orange juice according to taste).

The people in the south of Portugal have most imaginative names for their sweets and cakes.

There is *Bolo de bom gosto do Convento da Esperança*, *Toucinho do céu* (heavenly bacon), nun's belly, angel's breasts, lover's cakes and many more.

*Colchão de noiva*, meaning the bride's mattress or bed sheet, is yet another unlikely title for a traditional sweet.

# BRIDE'S BED SHEET *COLCHÃO DE NOIVA*

| | |
|---|---|
| *20 egg white* | *200 g icing sugar* |
| *2 cups ovos moles* | *icing sugar to sprinkle* |
| *some raspberry jam* | |

Whisk the egg white and sugar until very stiff. (You must be able to cut through with a knife).

Cover a baking tray with grease-proof paper. Spread the egg white mixture evenly on to the tray.

Dry in a warm oven, of no more than 80 - 100 degrees, for approximately 20 minutes.

While still warm, cut into rectangles and spread with *ovos moles*, then cover with a second egg white rectangle.

Sprinkle with lots of icing sugar and put a blob of raspberry jam into the centre.

# A DAY IN THE FIELDS

Back from the beaches and rocky coastline, where tourism and road construction have still left some space, the farming community of the Algarve tends the land that stretches all the way to the mountains.

They work on sand or on heavy dark red earth. There are fields full of stone that require considerable effort to convert them into vineyards or orchards or small vegetable plots.

The rural population used to be a three-tier society. There were landowners, small farmers and, on the lowest rung, day labourers who worked for others but usually owned or leased a small plot close to their home for their own use.

Much of this social structure has been kept to this day. There are still quite a few landowners who cultivate large sections of the Algarve, mainly with citrus.

The small farmers still keep a few animals and work on a few hectares of land if they have not already sold it to a developer for a tourist project.

During our explorations for this book we met three women who have known life in the countryside and work in the fields from early childhood, but from very different perspectives. Over the next few pages we would like to introduce Maria Lizette Conceição Santos from Galé, Maria do Carmo Alves Cabrita Severino from Algoz and Isabel Conceição Correia from Guia.

Isabel's parents were farm workers or, more precisely, day labourers - poor people who hardly earned enough to keep them alive despite growing their own produce on a piece of land close to where they lived. When times were really hard, food would be prepared in the field itself from ingredients that may seem strange to us now.

Isabel remembers the following meal vividly. She says she will never forget its taste. She has called it *Cardo do campo* and it consists mainly of thistles.

The leaves of a thistle were torn from its stem and cooked in water. They were squeezed - mainly to get rid of the bitter taste - then chopped finely and mixed with a few eggs into a porridge, or cooked with potatoes if there were any.

Isabel has also contributed this recipe for a very simple soup which used to be taken to the workers in the fields.

# FARMER'S SOUP *SOPA DO CAMPO*

| | |
|---|---|
| 2 tbsp flour | 1 tbsp oil |
| 1 radish | 1 carrot |
| 1 garlic clove | 1 celery |
| 3/4 litre beef stock | 1/4 litre milk |

Brown the flour in oil and add stock. Cook for 5 minutes and put to one side.

Peel radish and carrot and grate into rough pieces. Press the garlic and cut the celery into fine pieces.

Add to the stock, add salt and pepper to taste and bring to the boil. Add the milk and serve with bread.

The bread traditionally used was round, flat, dough bread that would be baked on hot stones by the fire in the field.

Most of the time, however, landowners would have the meal prepared and taken out to their workers. Much to the distress of Maria do Carmo when she was a child, her mother would prepare her favourite dish, *Papas*, for the farm workers, but local custom dictated that Maria, being the landowner's daughter, was not allowed to share the meal with them.

Maria do Carmo's father grew almonds, figs, olives, wheat and corn. It was not a very large property, but it was still quite sizable and social distinctions between owners and workers were well established.

Maria do Carmo would have gone without the *papas* she loved so much had it not been for an old farm-hand known to her as Tio Zé, Uncle Joe. He had worked for her family for many years and it was he who would start his own little fire in the field and cook Maria's favourite dish for her.

So what exactly is *Papas*? It is a dish which the Moors brought to the Algarve from North Africa and which is also known by the Arabic name *xerém* or *xarem*. Here is how you can make it.

## CORNMEAL PORRIDGE *PAPAS OR XERÉM*

| | |
|---|---|
| *200 g cornflour* | *250 g smoked bacon* |
| *1 1/2 litre beef stock* | *1 onion* |
| *salt, pepper* | |

Cut the bacon into very small cubes and lightly cook until brown. Remove the crackling from the fat but keep aside.

Cut the onion finely and brown in fat. Add the stock and bring to the boil.

Gently add cornflour and continue to stir. Bring again to the boil and add salt and pepper. Continue to simmer and stir until the mixture has thickened into a porridge.

Sprinkle with crackling and serve hot.

There are quite a few varieties of *Papas*. One can for example use *chouriços* instead of, or together with, bacon. Another way of preparation is Cornmeal porridge with sardines (see page 132).

We recommend a fish stock for *Papas* with seafood.

Here is another possibility:
Chop the onion into small pieces and fry in 1 tbsp of lard and 3 tbsp of olive oil.

Skin a tomato, remove pips and cut into small cubes. Finely chop a sprig of parsley and add to the onion mixture. Mix into *Papas* mixture and bring to the boil just once.

Such simple soups and stews used to be the staple food in the Algarve - other than bread and roasted figs, of course, which everybody who worked in the fields would carry with them in large quantities. *Sopa de pedra,* stone soup, was such a meal and with it goes a story known in many versions.

Once upon a time there was an old man (a different story speaks of 'a travelling monk') who went begging in the Algarve from door to door, farmhouse to farmhouse. One evening he reached a lonely farmhouse in the hills and the people there gave him shelter.

He was very poor but very proud. When he asked in the kitchen if he could cook himself a little soup, they agreed. But the farmer's wife was most surprised to see the old man reach into his bag and take out a few stones.

He put the stones into his cooking pot, poured water over them and put the pot on the fire.

How could the old man possibly think that these stones and water would make a good soup?

"Be patient for a little while," answered the old man and left. Feeling sorry for him, the farmer's wife took whatever vegetables she had in her own pots and added a little of each to the stones.

In a different version of this story the old man supposedly answered that the stones were all he needed, but he would like just a few things to cook with them.

Whatever the story, the result was the same. Stone soup was born and it exists to this day. *Sopa de pedra* is an ideal way to use up left-overs. Here is one recipe:

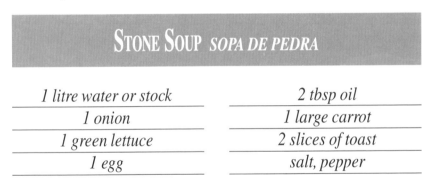

## STONE SOUP *SOPA DE PEDRA*

| | |
|---|---|
| *1 litre water or stock* | *2 tbsp oil* |
| *1 onion* | *1 large carrot* |
| *1 green lettuce* | *2 slices of toast* |
| *1 egg* | *salt, pepper* |

Heat the oil in a saucepan, cut onion into slices and brown in the oil.

Cut lettuce and carrot into small pieces, add to the onion and pour water or stock over it.

Break toast into small crumbs and add to soup. Cook for about 10 minutes, add salt and pepper to taste.

Whisk the egg and pour gently into soup.

This stew could be improved by adding chicken, pork, beef, or almost anything that grows in the fields of the Algarve. Along with the traditional grains of wheat, maize and sometimes barley, fruit, nuts and all kinds of vegetables are grown for home consumption and for sale in the local markets.

In her childhood and youth, Maria Lizette Conceição Santos from Galé witnessed the gradual improvement in her parents' finances. Her father was a small farmer who grew mostly wheat, tomatoes and vegetables and kept a few animals: a cow, pigs, chickens and rabbits. Initially they took their produce on foot to the market, but as they were hard-working and industrious they were able to buy a donkey, then a mule and eventually even a small car.

Today the source of rabbit tends to be from the hunter rather than from the hutch. Nevertheless, Maria Lizette's way of cooking rabbit has not changed.

## RABBIT VALE DE PARRA *COELHO VALE DE PARRA*

| | |
|---|---|
| *1 rabbit, 800 - 1000g* | *1/4 litre red wine* |
| *5 juniper berries* | *2 cloves* |
| *1/2 bay leaf* | *1/2 cup of chopped onion* |
| *1/2 cup of small bacon cubes* | *2 chopped garlic cloves* |
| *1 sprig of rosemary* | *1/2 cup of cream* |
| *salt, pepper* | |

Clean and gut the rabbit and cut into four parts. Make a marinade of red wine, juniper berries, cloves, bay leaf, garlic, onion, rosemary, salt and pepper. Cover the rabbit with marinade and stand for one day.

Brown bacon in a saucepan, dry the rabbit meat and add to the bacon. Pour the marinade over it and simmer until done. Add cream to sauce and serve with savoy cabbage and boiled potatoes.

Maria Lizette's father's farm was small but she and her brothers and sisters had to help out. She learned all about farm work from a very early age and still puts this knowledge to good use today.

She does not spray pesticides on her crops and she grows different crops side by side, a good protection against parasites. On her small piece of land, which she works on her own, she continues to grow a variety of vegetables just as her father and grandfather did before her.

Every year at the end of January she plants tomato seedlings, surrounding them with *piteiras,* Agave leaves, for protection. When she sows her broad beans, green peas and chick-peas in January or February, she will throw a few chicken feathers on to the ground. This is a touch of magic which also warns birds that it might be quite dangerous to steal the seeds.

Many ancient farming methods remain alive. On the Algarve's west coast, fields are still ploughed by yolked oxen. In the north-east, some farmers still sow their wheat by hand and harvest with their sickles. The mule pulling its ploughshare is also still a fairly common sight.

As there are several harvests throughout the year, the ground is ploughed, harrowed and hoed accordingly. However, all farmers plough their fields after the first heavy rain in October when the earth can be broken up easily. By the time of the Day of the Immaculate Conception (8th December) the country is green again. Nowadays, of course, many farmers use tractors, but to pull the very first plough through the fields with one's own animals is a superstition which raises hopes of a good harvest.

Even though there are machines available, there is one tool to work the ground that can be found in every single farmhouse: the hoe. Algarvians hardly ever use a spade. They use the hoe for everything. They will dig with it, harvest with it and collect the potatoes from the ground with it. There are hoes of many different shapes and sizes and they all have their own names.

Other than the harrow, plough and hoe there is a special agricultural tool called the *trilho*. This is a threshing roller that looks like a high-seated toboggan and is usually drawn by a mule across the *eira*, the threshing floor. Below the seat there are cylindrical rollers with iron spikes that separate the chaff from the grain.

You may notice a small heap of stones in the field. This a fertility symbol that the Algarvians have adopted from Moorish times. Algarve farmers will pray for a good harvest in similar fashion to their Arabian counterparts. The Algarvians also learnt from the Moors how to irrigate their fields. Water was and still is drawn up from deep wells and then fed through canals and aqueducts to furrows among vegetable crops and fruit trees.

Even farmers like Maria Lizette, though, are adopting modern materials for growing their vegetables. She raises her melons under plastic covers and she will tie magnetic tape from old audio cassettes around her peas to frighten off the birds.

Maria Lizette has a special home recipe for peas.

## PEAS ALGARVE-STYLE *ERVILHAS À MODA DO ALGARVE*

| | |
|---|---|
| *500 g fresh peas from the pod* | *1 cup chopped tomatoes* |
| *1 cup chopped onions* | *2 tbsp olive oil* |
| *1/2 litre stock* | *4 thin slices lean belly pork* |
| *100 g linguiça* | *4 eggs* |
| *1 tbsp chopped parsley* | *salt, pepper* |

Heat 1 tbsp of oil in a saucepan and brown the onions and tomatoes. Add salt, pepper and the stock; then add peas and cover. Simmer until soft.

Lightly salt belly pork and fry on both sides with the remainder of the oil. Cut *linguiça* (or any other smoked garlic sausage) into slices and add to meat.

Serve peas in a bowl and sprinkle with parsley. Place meat and sausage slices on top. Fry the eggs (over and under if you prefer) and cover meat with fried eggs. Serve with fried potatoes.

# SOMETHING
# ABOUT OLIVES

They are green, purple or black and they all have different names depending on their degree of ripeness and method of storage. If you venture into the interior of the Algarve you can see the trees on which they grow. Olives trees are stocky and gnarled, bent from the wind. They can be as old as a thousand years.

Since ancient times they have grown around the Mediterranean and in Portugal where various traditions have developed as to how to use them.

In the Algarve, olive trees flower in the spring and are harvested by the end of September. The Algarvians themselves no longer press olives, unless it is for their own home consumption, as there are not sufficient quantities to make this effort commercially worthwhile.

Most other regions of Portugal do press olives commercially and that is why you will find special shelves in supermarkets with a wide choice of olive oils, some of them being more expensive than a good bottle of wine. The best is the so-called "virgin" oil from the very first, careful pressing.

What the Algarvians have maintained is the traditional way of preserving and storing olives.

When the olives are still green and being picked, they are called *azeitonas britadas*. The fruit is slightly crushed with a stone or a piece of wood to break the flesh but not the pip. It is covered with water and stored in a clay pot for about ten days. This storage water must be renewed every day.

The most important factor is the *salmoura* preservation liquid. Take sea salt, as it is found in the salt pans of the Algarve, and mix with water. Then season with one or two bay leaves, a broken clove of garlic, a sprig of thyme and oregano (for about two litres of water).

Put the olives into a clean clay or wooden container. Fill the container with *salmoura*. The olives must be completely covered with the *salmoura*; remember that some of the liquid will evaporate. Close the lid tightly. After the olives have been in the brine for about a month, the *britadas* are ready to eat.

Black olives should not to be crushed. They are scored vertically three times with a knife. This is why they have the name *azeitonas de facadinhas* (*faca* means knife). After this they are preserved just like the *britadas*.

Specially selected, large ripe olives are kept in water for a month. A little sea salt has already been added to the water which is only changed every two or three days. These olives are called *azeitonas de água*. The *salmoura* is the same as for the *britadas*.

The purple coloured olives have three names when they are prepared the way Maria de Carmo from Algoz has shown us. They are *azeitonas de sal*, *azeitonas de sapateiro* or *azeitonas de casamento* (wedding olives).

Initially they are kept between layers of sea salt for three or four weeks in a clay pot or, preferably, a basket. The container is shut with a piece of wood or clay which is weighted down by a heavy stone. Afterwards they are washed in luke-warm water and seasoned with sweet paprika, caraway seeds, parsley, garlic and vinegar. They taste particularly aromatic. They are eaten with bread and sheep's cheese from the *serras*.

Summer

Summer approaches bringing with it abundance. Market stalls are full of fruit. A big range of fresh vegetables is on offer and the fishermen will now make their most productive catches. Only the wildflowers in the south of Portugal seem to hold their breath because of the great heat. They wait until the autumn rain to blossom again. But there are still innumerable irrigated gardens to ensure that the profusion of flowers does not cease.

But summer also will brings the big squeeze. They push their way through towns and villages and settle down on beaches: the new invaders, the occupying forces of today, are the tourists.

Amid the hectic commotion, many tourist scarcely notice the inhabitants of the country in which they are spending their holidays. In many cases they want to enjoy the sun and beaches without getting to know a different way of life. In restaurants they choose familiar dishes from the menu, not daring to try the unfamiliar. It is a great shame because the Algarve and its cuisine have so much to offer.

If you do want to try something different, to get away for a moment from the heat and hustle and bustle of the summer and learn about the real Algarvians, then you must go to the old Café Aliança right in the centre of Faro. Here, amid the stuccoed ceilings, old photographs and wrought iron tables, you will find the true locals. Ask for a *bica* and a glass of water, or a *bica cheia*, and let go for a moment while listening to the conversation around you. Where exactly is this Café Aliança? You will find it on a corner opposite the Manuel Bivar garden, near the harbour.

Or why don't you visit one of the roadside snack-bars in the *serras* where the lorry drivers stop for a break. They are good places to observe ordinary people from a very different culture.

# SUMMER RECIPES

Summertime is the season of immense heat in the Algarve.

It is also the time when the most delectable fish are caught in great quantities and when many fruits are ready for harvesting.

Summertime is the time of great profusion.

The following seasonal recipes match the climate and what is on offer in the markets.

*Gaspacho* is a cold soup. In origin it is usually thought of as Spanish, but this is not necessarily so. In Portugal too, particularly in the southern regions of the Alentejo and the Algarve, *gaspacho* has a long tradition. Here it is called *arjamolho* or *algeramolho*.

In the heat of the summer it is a wonderful refreshment.

# GASPACHO *ARJAMOLHO*

| | |
|---|---|
| *1 green and 1 red capsicum* | *1 onion* |
| *1 cucumber* | *2 tomatoes* |
| *1 tbsp tomato purée* | *1/2 cup oil* |
| *3 tbsp bread crumbs* | *1 litre water* |
| *2 tbsp vinegar* | *salt, pepper* |
| *piri-piri or Sambel Olek* | *sauce or purée* |
| *1 cup toasted bread cubes* | |

Keep a third of the vegetables aside, chop the rest and purée in a blender.

Put into a large bowl and add water, vinegar, oil, tomato purée and bread crumbs. Season to taste with salt, pepper and piri-piri sauce.

Keep in the refrigerator for 3 to 4 hours and season again.

Cut the remaining vegetables into fine cubes. Serve vegetables and bread crumbs separately in small bowls. Serve the actual *gaspacho* from a large bowl. Everyone helps themselves while eating.

As an alternative to piri-piri, Sambal Olek are readily available Indonesian spices. Another alternative, or supplement, is *massa de pimentos* (see page 60).

There is another cold Portuguese soup that refreshes in summer. The traditional recipe has been altered slightly here as the original is not quite as substantial as northern Europeans might like.

## COLD MILK SOUP *SOPA DE LEITE*

| | |
|---|---|
| 1/2 litre milk | 1/4 litre cream |
| 1/4 litre yoghurt | 2 hard boiled eggs, finely |
| 2 slices cooked ham | chopped |
| 100 g finely ground almonds | 2 garlic cloves |
| 1 tbsp chopped green coriander | salt |

Crush the garlic with a pestle and mortar. Add almonds, salt and coriander and make a paste. Put into a large bowl and add milk, yoghurt and cream. Mix altogether. Add the eggs and ham and cool in the refrigerator for a few hours.

## SOUP WITH FISH DUMPLINGS
### *SOPA COM ALMONDEGAS DE PEIXE*

| **(for stock)** | 1 kg fish scraps |
|---|---|
| 1 onion | 1 garlic clove |
| 1 tomato | 1 celery with leaves |
| 1 carrot | 1/2 tsp thyme |
| 1/2 bay leaf | 1 cup dry white wine |
| 3/4 litre water | salt, pepper, a little oil |

Wash the fish.

Dice the vegetables and fry with chopped herbs in a little oil.

Add fish, water and wine to the vegetables and cook for about 30 minutes.

Pass through a sieve and add salt and pepper to taste.

| **(for soup)** | *1 litre fish stock* |
|---|---|
| *200 g fish without skin and bones* | *1 egg* |
| | *1 tsp lemon juice* |
| *1 tsp chopped parsley* | *1 tbsp flour* |
| *1/2 tsp curry powder* | *salt, pepper* |

Purée the fish in a blender.

Mix the purée with the egg, lemon juice, parsley and spices; bind with flour.

Use a teaspoon to mould little dumplings and allow to simmer in the hot fish stock for 5 to 8 minutes.

In a small road just off the fishing harbour of Armação de Pera, José Francisco Rodrigues Vieira owns a little restaurant called Zé Leiteiro. There is no menu but you can eat grilled fish just caught by the fishermen.

The fish is served with salad and bread or potatoes. The price is fixed and you can eat as much as you like.

José has given us the following recipe for eel. Eel can still be found in the Algarve in the rivers flowing into the sea - in the

Guadiana, and in the Alcantarilha and the Espiche when they are flowing in winter.

## EEL SOUP *ENSOPADO DE ENGUIAS*

| | |
|---|---|
| 1 kg of small eels | 1 finely diced capsicum |
| 2 tomatoes, skinned and diced | 1 tbsp oil |
| 1 onion, chopped | 1 cup fish stock |
| 1 tbsp red wine | salt, pepper |

Clean and gut the eels; take the heads off and cut into five to eight centimetre long pieces.

Heat the oil in a flat saucepan and add the onion, capsicum and tomatoes. Simmer until soft.

Add the stock and the red wine. Season to taste with salt and pepper and bring to the boil.

Add the eel and allow to simmer for about 10 minutes. Serve with fresh bread.

Rod and line fishermen at Galé beach stand on and between the rocks at high tide and wait for a fish to take their bait.

Meanwhile, one of the anglers takes some driftwood and makes a small fire. He is equipped with a couple of roof tiles from a construction site. When a fish is caught, this is how it is cooked.

# FISH IN THE TILE *FATAÇA NA TELHA*

| | |
|---|---|
| *1 sea bass or similar fish of about 1 - 1 1/2 kg weight* | *1 tbsp lemon juice* |
| *2 tbsp oil* | *1 chopped onion* |
| *200 g bacon* | *2 tbsp chopped parsley* |
| | *salt, pepper* |

Clean and gut the fish and make incisions on both sides with a knife. Mix the onion with oil, lemon juice, parsley, salt and pepper and rub this all over the fish, inside and outside.

Put layers of bacon on to the inside of a tile, put the fish on top, cover it with more slices of bacon and close it with a second tile. Bury in hot ash or hot coal, or grill on the barbecue.

Serve with green lettuce and baked potatoes.

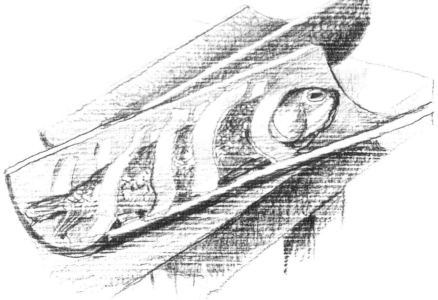

We have seen a similar procedure described in a Portuguese cookery book, but specifying herring rather than sea bass.

And what is to be done back home if there is no Portuguese roof tile at hand? Take an earthenware pot and cook as above.

## GALÉ CAKE *BOLO GALÉ*

| | |
|---|---|
| *250 g flour* | *150 g sugar* |
| *100 g butter* | *100 g ground almonds* |
| *100 g finely chopped walnuts* | *1 tsp cinnamon* |
| *1 tbsp honey* | *pinch of ground cloves* |
| *1/2 cup red wine* | *1 cup doce de chila* |

Mix sugar, flour, nuts, spices, honey, red wine and cold pieces of butter into a short pastry.

Allow to rest in the refrigerator for about 30 minutes.

Roll out the dough thinly and lay out some of it in a well greased, round, flat baking tin, leaving a small rim. Cover with *doce de chila*, pumpkin jam.

Cut the remainder of the dough into thin strips and lay in a criss-cross pattern over the top. Bake in a pre-heated oven of 200 degrees for about 20 to 30 minutes.

The preparation of *doce de chila* is described on page 27. In Portugal it is also available in the supermarkets.

*Fatias de Tomar* means "dipped slices".

They are usually eaten as an alternative to cake with a cup of coffee.

## FATIAS DE TOMAR

| | |
|---|---|
| *20 egg yolks* | *2 tbsp flour* |
| *500 g sugar* | *1/2 litre orange juice* |

Whisk the egg yolks with the flour until frothy and fill into a well greased baking tin and close with a lid.

Bake in the oven at about 100 - 120 degrees until hard, then cut into slices.

Mix orange juice with sugar and cook until it has become syrup. Dip *fatias* into syrup and allow to cool.

# PIRI-PIRI
# AND
# MASSA DE PIMENTOS

*Frango piri-piri* appears on just about every menu. *Piri-piri* features in numerous recipes as an essential ingredient. Curiosity is aroused. What exactly is this *piri-piri ?*

It is a sauce made from small, red hot peppers of the genus paprika. You can buy them in the markets, often strung together like beads on a chain.

They are made into a sauce, sometimes with pips and sometimes without, which may or not be ground, mixed with salt water and ....

The "and" is classified information. There are many possible additional ingredients and blends, but they are jealously guarded secrets. You can, for example, add vinegar. If it is still not hot enough you may add ground pepper.

*Piri-piri* is rubbed into the chicken prior to baking or grilling, or served separately at the table.

*Piri-piri* originated in Portugal's former African colonies. It was brought back, along with other African recipes, and popularised in mainland Portugal by those who evacuated the colonies at the time of their turbulent independence in the 1970s. In the face of unemployment in Portugal, many of those arriving from Africa set up their own restaurants.

The Algarvians have a few specific recipes for their own hot sauces variously known as *calda de pimenta*, *calda pimentão* or *massa de pimentos*. They serve the same purpose as the *piri-piri* and accompany many dishes.

## MASSA DE PIMENTOS

| | |
|---|---|
| *1 kilo ripe, red peppers of medium size* | *1 cup of salt* |
| *2 cloves of garlic* | *1 cup olive oil* |

Wash the peppers and chop. Mix with salt - with or without

pips as desired. Leave to stand in a closed earthenware pot for eight to ten days.

Purée the chopped peppers and garlic in a blender. Give it one more stir before filling screw top jars to no more than two-thirds. Top up with olive oil.

Always use a clean spoon when serving and make sure that the *massa de pimento* is covered with oil to prevent mould forming.

Nowadays, *piri-piri* peppers are grown in the Algarve. Ready-made sauces are available in the supermarkets and home-made *massa de pimentos* can be found in the vegetable markets.

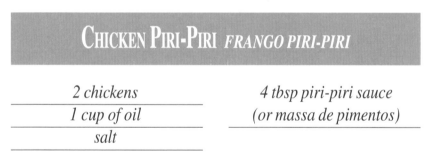

## CHICKEN PIRI-PIRI *FRANGO PIRI-PIRI*

| | |
|---|---|
| *2 chickens* | *4 tbsp piri-piri sauce* |
| *1 cup of oil* | *(or massa de pimentos)* |
| *salt* | |

Cut the chicken into pieces no more than ten centimetres long. Put into a bowl and mix well with *piri-piri* sauce or *massa de pimentos* which may have to be thinned.

Cover and leave to stand for one to two hours. Add salt to taste.

Use a frying pan to heat the oil to a high temperature, then put in the chicken pieces side by side and cook until brown.

Serve with salad and bread.

# A SUMMER MENU FROM
# THE DOIS IRMÃOS RESTAURANT
# IN FARO

The decor and the menu of this restaurant may give the impression that it appeals specifically to foreign tourists, but in fact it attracts many Portuguese customers. This is because of the high quality of the Portuguese cuisine on offer. Another reason could be the tradition of the establishment itself.

It is the oldest in Faro. In 1927 it was founded by two brothers, hence the name. Today, customers are pampered in what was originally a welder's workshop.

The building used to include stables for horses, which meant that travellers stopped here with the intention of staying overnight.

The restaurant has existed in its present form since 1976 but has recently been renovated. If you want to eat here, you will have to look for the Praça Ferreira de Almeida and turn into the Largo Terreiro do Bispo.

The Dois Irmãos is managed by Henrique Maria Lourenço Brazuna. Unlike most other restaurateurs in the Algarve, he has had a thorough professional training in Switzerland and elsewhere. The owner of Dois Irmãos is his father.

The chef is João Martel, a true Algarvian from Vila Real de St.º António. He has been a chef for 27 years, the past 16 years of them at the Dois Irmãos. His proposed summer menu concentrates on seafood. This is not surprising as the quality of fish in the Algarve is particularly good throughout the summer season.

His menu: Fish soup,
Sardines Portuguese-style,
Cataplana de Dois Irmãos,
Almond cake.

## FISH SOUP *SOPA DE PEIXE*

| | |
|---|---|
| *500 g cod* | *150 g small, star-shaped noodles* |
| *2 tomatoes* | |
| *1/2 capsicum* | *1 onion* |
| *1/2 cup oil* | *sprigs of green coriander* |
| *1 cup mussels* | *1 litre water* |
| *salt, pepper* | *1 tbsp lemon juice* |

Gut the fish and wash. Put into a saucepan with cold water and bring to the boil. Cook for 8 to 10 minutes.

Take the fish out of the liquid and pass the stock through a fine sieve.

Chop the onion finely and brown in the oil. Remove the pips from tomatoes and capsicum, cut into small pieces and add to the onion. Pour the fish stock over the vegetables.

Add noodles and cook for about 15 to 20 minutes. Just before they are done, add the mussels. Add salt, pepper and lemon juice to taste.

Remove the bones and skin from the fish and cut into small portions. Add to the soup and sprinkle with chopped coriander.

Chef João Martel recommends cod for this soup because of its strong white meat which does not fall apart when cooked. If you wish to use this recipe at home, you should select a similar fish.

Visitors to the Algarve must really not depart without having sampled, at least once, the sardines grilled in the way the fishermen eat them. Sardines taste best in the summer months of June, July and August. As a starter, here is an alternative.

## SARDINES PORTUGUESE-STYLE *SARDINHAS À PORTUGUESA*

| | |
|---|---|
| *16 sardines* | *1 green capsicum* |
| *2 tomatoes* | *2 onions* |
| *2 garlic cloves* | *1/2 litre oil* |
| *1 glass white wine* | *salt, pepper* |
| *500 g potatoes* | *1 tbsp chopped parsley* |

Chop capsicum, tomatoes, onions and garlic very finely and cook in wine until you have a sauce. Add salt and pepper to taste.

Scale sardines and gut. Cut off heads. Fry in hot oil for 2 to 3 minutes, then take out of the oil. Add peeled and quartered potatoes to the oil and fry. Place sardines into a bowl and cover with sauce. Surround with potatoes and sprinkle with parsley.

If you wish to cook the following dish you will need a *cataplana*. This is a simple steam cooker that can also be used as a frying pan. The *cataplana* is a traditional Algarvian household gadget which consists of two pan-like halves held together by a clasp. It has two handles and two clips that tightly close it. It is made of an alloy metal, although you can buy luxury versions made of copper. If you want to buy a *cataplana* for later use, it is preferable to buy in a household shop and not a souvenir shop.

Several dishes can be prepared in a *cataplana*. Here is one of them.

## CATAPLANA Á DOIS IRMÃOS

| | |
|---|---|
| *400 g pork filet* | *1 kg ameijoas (clams)* |
| *six slices of lean bacon, about 2 cm thick* | *12 large crabs* |
| | *2 tomatoes* |
| *1 green capsicum* | *1 onion* |
| *1 tsp sweet paprika* | *2 bay leaves* |
| *5 or 6 garlic cloves* | *2 glasses white wine* |
| *sprigs of green coriander* | *50 g pork lard (or 1 cup of oil)* |
| *salt, pepper* | |

Cut the pork into large cubes and season with paprika, bay leaves, crushed garlic, salt and pepper. Leave to stand for one day.

Wash the mussels very carefully, soak in salt water and leave to stand.

Open the *cataplana* and place on the stove. Heat the lard or oil in the *cataplana* and fry the pork, then pour the fat away.

Increase the heat, add mussels and stir thoroughly.

Cut tomatoes, onions and capsicum into slices and place on mussels. Progressively build up circular layers using one slice of bacon and two crabs per layer.

Pour wine over the top and sprinkle with chopped green coriander. Close the lid of the *cataplana* and cook on a strong heat for approximately 10 minutes. Gently shake the *cataplana* several times.

In the Dois Irmãos the *cataplana* is set into a bed of sea salt on an oval plate and only opened at the table.

João Martel revealed the secret of how you can tell without opening the *cataplana* if all ingredients are well cooked. He knocks the metal with his spoon. If there is a light sound the mussels are open; if there is a deep sound, they are not yet ready.

The *cataplana* has another advantage: While eating, one can keep the lid closed so the food remains hot.

By the way, if you don't have a *cataplana* you can use an ordinary saucepan, but you must remember to keep the lid closed.

It is quite customary in the Algarve to serve cake, such as almond cake, as a dessert. The preparations for *ovos moles* as required for this recipe are described on page 26.

## ALMOND CAKE *TORTA DE AMÊNDOA ALGARVIA*

| | |
|---|---|
| *250 g ground almonds (unpeeled)* | *8 eggs* |
| *300 g flour* | *200 g sugar* |
| *1 tbsp ground lemon peel* | *1 tsp baking powder* |
| *2 cups ovos moles for filling and topping* | *100 g butter* |
| | *whole almonds to garnish* |

Whisk eggs and sugar to a froth. Mix flour and baking powder into it. Add the ground almonds and the lemon peel.

Add melted butter and stir into a creamy texture.

Grease a flat baking tin and fill with dough, no higher than approximately 2 centimetres. Spread flat.

In a pre-heated oven, bake at 180 - 200 degrees for 15 to 20 minutes.

Lay the cake on to grease-proof paper and cover with *ovos moles*. Fold into a roll.

Cover the completed roll again with *ovos moles* and garnish with whole almonds.

# BAKING DAY

When you see one of those old farmhouses in the Algarve you invariably find beside it an old stone oven. Long ago, when the Algarve country people were mostly self-supporting, it was here that they baked their bread.

Every farmer, regardless of whether he was rich or poor, had his own bread oven. Every housewife wanted to bake her own bread.

These bread ovens were built with natural stone and had a thick rendering, usually made of clay. There was a small opening in the front and a chimney at the back. Both could be closed as required.

Baking day was once a week and generally a wheat bread was baked using flour, salt, water and *levedura* ( yeast).

Usually a small portion of the dough was kept for the next baking day, making the addition of fresh yeast unnecessary.

About 14 or 15 loaves of bread were baked for one family per week. Families tended to be large and bread was one of the staple foods. It was used as a base for soups and was served with fish and meat dishes.

Loaves would keep for about 10 days. They used to be much harder than the ones baked today. The reason for this may have been the technique of baking, or that bakers used less water.

Little cakes, such as *costas* (small ribs), were baked on the same day as the loaves. They were made as sweet pastries, or with crackling or spices.

Large cakes were also baked. These are called *brindeiros* or *bolos do fundo do alguidar* (cakes from the bottom of the bowl in which the dough is raised). They were baked with the remaining bread dough, but went into the oven first to check if the heat of the bricks was sufficient to bake the bread after the glowing charcoal had been removed.

Here is a recipe for the little cakes as dictated to us by Maria do Carmo from Algoz.

## *COSTAS*

*1 kg bread dough, from the baker  (as a substitute you can start the sour dough yourself by using a ready-made or pizza dough mixture)*

| | | |
|---|---|---|
| 2 tbsp pork lard or margarine | 2 tbsp oil | |
| 2 tsp ground cinnamon | 1 tsp ground lemon peel | |
| 1 tsp aniseed | 2 tbsp honey | |
| 1 cup sugar | some flour | |
| some icing sugar | | |

Gradually knead all ingredients into the ready-made dough.
Take small portions and shape into small round, flat cakes. Cover with a cloth and stand to rest for some time.

Put on a greased baking tray and bake in a pre-heated oven at 180 degrees for 20 to 25 minutes until golden brown. While they are still warm, sprinkle icing sugar on top.

In days gone by, when baking was finished the oven and its heat were used to roast sweet potatoes or dry figs. Today all this has changed. Families do not bake their bread themselves anymore. Bread ovens in front of houses fall into disrepair or are used for different purposes. Nowadays the commercial baker produces the bread.

We visited Isabel Maria Conceição Correia in Guia where she and her husband have been running their own little bakery for the last 12 years.

Today they make the same sort of bread with the same ingredients as in former times. It is a light, long or round wheat bread. To this day, a small portion of the dough is kept in order to start the following day's baking.

The flour is delivered in huge bags, but it does not come from this region. Algarve windmills - the few that still exist - do not grind flour anymore.

When buying flour in Portugal, study the label to check whether or not baking powder has been added.

Other than standard bread, Isabel Conceição and her husband make bread rolls and a full-grained so-called "health bread". They also roast wheat flour in their oven and use it for making the following drink.

## CALDO DE FARINHA TORRADA

| | |
|---|---|
| *2 heaped tbsp flour* | *1/2 litre milk* |
| *1/2 litre water* | *1 tsp vanilla sugar* |
| *1 tbsp ordinary sugar* | *1 tbsp ground lemon peel* |

Roast the flour by gently stirring in a pot until dark brown, then remove from the heat.

Add the vanilla sugar (as a substitute take a pinch of *vanilina em cristais*). Add the sugar and top up with water. Stand to soak for five minutes.

Add the milk and finely ground lemon peel and stir.

(Orange juice may be used instead of water and milk).

*Caldo de farinha* can be drunk either hot or cold. It has lots of calories, but is very healthy.

Traditional baking practices have been maintained in the

little bakery in Guia. The Correias start their oven with a fire made of wood and then add some almond shells to enhance the taste of the bread. Local bakers used to burn almond, olive or fig wood to improve the flavour. Corn of the cob was sometimes added to increase the heat.

Isabel Conceição Correia comes from a very poor family. She remembers her childhood well. Her parents worked in the fields near Silves. When they didn't have enough money for flour, they had to find a substitute. Sometimes her grandmother used beans from the carob tree (*alfarrobeira*) to bake bread.

The carob tree grows everywhere in the Algarve. When dried, the beans (*alfarrobas*) can be eaten on their own or with a piece of bread, but mostly they are used for pig fodder.

They are also used in the production of chocolate, coffee and sweets. The seeds contain a glue-like substance that is still used in the textile, leather, cosmetics and pharmaceutical industries.

The following carob recipe, adapted from the original, produces bread with quite an interesting taste.

## CAROB BREAD *PÃO DE ALFARROBA*

| | |
|---|---|
| *250 g carob beans* | *1 kg flour* |
| *water* | *30 g yeast* |
| *some wheat bran* | *salt* |

Mix the yeast in luke warm water and some flour and let stand.

Grind the dry carob beans very finely and mix with the yeast, flour, water, salt and a small amount of wheat bran, up to one cupful to taste.

Knead into a dough. Cover and stand for 3 or 4 hours.

Shape into a loaf and bake.

Isabel Conceição Correia in Guia has given us another recipe, this one for an Easter loaf. She still bakes it from time to time but does not sell it anymore. It is only available in the Algarve at Easter, as are the home-made, sugar-coated almonds which the Algarvians call *consoadas*.

People take Easter loaves along with them on country walks. They are good for picnics.

## EASTER LOAF *FOLAR DA PÁSCOA*

| | |
|---|---|
| *500 g flour* | *20 g yeast* |
| *1 cup milk* | *1 cup sugar* |
| *2 eggs* | *pinch of salt* |
| *1 tbsp ground lemon peel* | *125 g butter* |
| *1 tsp aniseed* | *4 eggs* |
| *butter to spread* | *icing sugar to sprinkle* |

Put flour into a bowl and make an indentation in the centre.

Put yeast into it, add some luke warm milk and mix altogether. Stand for 10 minutes.

Take the remainder of the flour, sugar, salt, melted butter, ground lemon peel, aniseed and 2 eggs and knead into a dough.

Cover and keep in a warm spot for 2 to 3 hours and allow to rise.

Grease a round baking mould and fill with dough.

Slightly pierce the shells of four eggs and press, with shell, into the dough in such a way that the tops are still visible.

The eggs may be covered with a criss-cross pattern of more dough. Spread melted butter over the top.

Bake in a pre-heated oven at approximately 180-200 degrees for 50 to 60 minutes.

When it is cool, sprinkle with icing sugar.


A final point about bread: If you really want to see how bread was baked here in the old days, go exploring in the Algarve hills. You may still find a farmhouse or two where baking is done in the traditional way.

# SOMETHING
# ABOUT
# FISH

Elisa Jesus Assunção Silva is about 50 years old and is usually to be found in the Albufeira fish market where she has worked for 14 years as a municipal employee.

She helps the fishermen to sell their catch to dealers by weighing and auctioning fish and organising whatever needs to be organised.

If anybody in Albufeira knows about fish, it's Elisa. That is not surprising. She has grown up with the sea. Her father was a fisherman and her brother still is.

The first thing we asked her was how does she tell if a fish is really fresh. It must be said, though, that if one compares the fish here with what appears in markets back home, every fish here is indeed "fresh".

To make sure, you have to check the colour of the eyes, she said. And, of course, fish should not smell. By touching a fish you can feel if the skin is still slippery or if it has been deep frozen. It is a good idea to check the gills too to see if they are well supplied with blood.

We also wanted to know her favourite type of fish and her favourite fish recipe. She said all fish were good and they all tasted as good as each other when either freshly grilled or fried. Of course she is right. We could not help noticing that whenever the fishermen return with their catch they invariably start a fire on the beach and grill one or two fish for themselves.

We would not let Elisa get away without revealing her favourite recipe and this is what she gave us: *Caldeirada*.

*Caldeirada* is a Portuguese speciality and each region has its own particular recipes. The best translation of *Caldeirada* is "fish stew". Various cookery books also speak of "fish goulash" or compare it with the French *bouillabaisse*, but that is not quite the same thing.

*Caldeirada* consists of different types of fish. Elisa chooses from those in season and it is important that the fish is fresh and its meat is firm and white.

## CALDEIRADA Á ALBUFEIRA

| | |
|---|---|
| *1 1/2 kg of fish -* | *500 g potatoes* |
| *3 or 4 different varieties* | *250 g onions* |
| *(sole, turbot, conger eel,* | *2 green capsicums* |
| *dogfish, perch)* | *1/4 litre water* |
| *1/4 litre dry white wine* | *1/2 bay leaf* |
| *2 garlic cloves* | *1/2 cup olive oil* |
| *1 tsp ground paprika* | *3 slices raw ham* |
| *salt, pepper* | *1 tbsp chopped parsley* |

Clean and gut the fish. Take out the bones and cut into fillets.

Peel the potatoes and cut into slices.

Skin tomatoes; take pips out of the capsicums; cut onions, capsicums and tomatoes into rings.

Heat the oil and brown the crushed garlic. Add bay leaf, water and wine.

Add the fish and simmer for approximately 20 minutes.

Pass the liquid through a fine sieve and season thoroughly.

Take an oven-proof dish and put potato slices into the base. Then layer repeatedly with onions, fish, capsicum and tomato rings. Pour fish stock over it and cover with slices of ham.

Seal with tin foil paper. Bake in the oven at 200 degrees for approximately 30 to 35 minutes.

Before serving, sprinkle chopped parsley.

The markets in the Algarve sell different types of fish for *Caldeirada* already cleaned and cut to size.

For many years in the Algarve, Elisa Jesus Assunção Silva has witnessed the development of fishing, a hard and sometimes dangerous occupation. She says that for the fishermen things have changed for the worse over the years. Today's catch is only a third of what was possible in former times. Then there is the huge Spanish fishing fleet to contend with, but the story of the Algarvians and the Spanish is a very different and long one.

Whilst expenses have steadily grown over the years, there has been very little increase in the price of fish and consequently in the profit for the fishermen. Elisa's brother, Emanuel, could speak about it if he wanted to.

For the past 12 years he has had his own boat. He tries to go out fishing every night, either on his own or with his nephew, but that is not always possible. He has to bear in mind certain basic rules: a lot of moonlight means little fish; if the sea is rough, stay at home; in the winter there is not much to catch anyway.

Emanuel has attached four lights to his boat. They are the same kind of lights that can be seen at night all along the coast-line of the Algarve. They are meant to attract the fish and other marine animals.

He catches mostly *lulas* and *chocos* (squid and cuttlefish), *sardinhas* (sardines), *cavalas* (mackerel), *carapaus* (horse mackerel) and whatever else swims into his nets. *Lulas* and *chocos* are the most lucrative and will fetch up to 1,300 escudos a kilo. Sardines will often fetch only a tenth of that.

Emanuel showed us his accounts after a night's fishing.

With only 8,600 escudos remaining he still had to pay the men at the beach who helped him to take his boat to the water. There was also the cost of petrol, oil, hooks, baits, wages .....

As for cooking the squid, we discovered two recipes.

## STUFFED SQUID *LULAS CHEIAS*

| | |
|---|---|
| 8 small squid | 1 tbsp lemon juice |
| 1/2 bay leaf | salt, pepper |
| 1 egg | 2 tbsp olive oil |
| 1 cup toasted white bread cubes | 1 tbsp chopped onions |
| 1 tbsp chopped parsley | 1 orange, not too sweet, peeled and |
| 1 tbsp fried bacon cubes | split into small pieces |
| 1/4 litre white wine | |

Whisk the egg and add bacon, toasted bread cubes and onions. Stir well. Season with salt and pepper to taste.

Stuff the cleaned squid with this paste. According to taste, you can chop the tentacles very finely and mix with the paste.

Hold the squid together with small tooth-picks.

Heat the oil in a saucepan. Add the orange pieces, the bay leaf and the lemon juice. Season with salt, pepper and parsley. Add the wine and allow to cook until thickened.

Put the stuffed squid side by side into the liquid, cover and stew for a few minutes. Do not allow to get hard.

Serve with tomato salad and white bread as a main dish.

# CUTTLEFISH WITH BEANS *CHOCOS COM FEIJÃO*

| | |
|---|---|
| *4 cuttlefish* | *2 tbsp olive oil* |
| *1 tbsp lemon juice* | *1 cup chopped tomato* |
| *1 tsp chopped garlic* | *2 cups cooked white beans* |
| *salt, pepper* | |

Gut the cuttlefish and wash.

Heat the oil in a saucepan and add the cuttlefish. Cover and cook for 2 to 3 minutes until done. Cut the cuttlefish into rings, 1 cm wide.

Add tomatoes and garlic to the still hot oil, shake once, season to taste with lemon juice, salt and pepper.

Fill into a bowl and mix with the cuttlefish rings and cooked white beans (you can also use *chicharros* or other beans). Allow to cool.

Serve with bread and white wine.

Here is a tip for those who do not like their squid or cuttlefish too hard. Cook them in salt water before preparing. Algarvians add one or two wine bottle corks. They claim the acid in the cork "softens" the squid.

The herbs of the Algarve are used to make a green sauce sometimes served with cooked fish.

# FISH WITH GREEN SAUCE *PESCADA NO MOLHO VERDE*

| | |
|---|---|
| 1 kg of cod | 1/2 litre water |
| 1 tbsp lemon juice | 1 tbsp green coriander |
| 1 tbsp parsley | 1 tsp dill |
| 1 cup double cream | 1 egg yolk |
| 20 g butter | salt, pepper |

Gut and fillet the cod.

Cut bones and skin into small pieces, add salt and cook for about 30 minutes.

Pass the broth through a fine sieve into a flat saucepan.

Add cream and cook until thickened to a sauce consistency.

Season with pepper and lemon juice and add the finely chopped herbs.

Algarvians do not use dill. They prefer *erva doce*, aniseed.

Add the fillet to the hot sauce and allow to simmer for about 10 minutes. Do not bring to the boil!

Add the egg yolk and the cream to bind the sauce.

Serve with rice.

The following recipe deals with the preparation of *carapaus*.

When they are small, *carapaus* are very similar to sardines. However, there are medium and large sized species as well. *Carapaus*, like sardines, taste best in the summer. They are not recommended before May. Emanuel told us a story about them and although we initially thought he was spinning a yarn, we believed it in the end. Here it is:

When you go shopping for *carapaus* you must touch every single one on the belly to check whether or not you can feel a piece of crab inside. If you do, don't buy the fish. The *carapaus* feed on a particular type of crab which is not always fully digested.

For our next recipe the *carapaus* need to be fresh and quite fat. Don't forget to feel their bellies before buying them!

## CARAPAUS COM CEBOLAS

| | |
|---|---|
| 1 kg medium-sized carapaus | 1 cup olive oil |
| 2 tbsp vinegar | 1 cup onion rings |
| 2 garlic cloves | salt, pepper |
| 1 tbsp chopped parsley | lemon juice |

Gut the fish and cut off their heads. Bring 1 litre of water with a lot of salt to the boil.

Cook the fish in this water for approximately 2 minutes. Then take them out.

Skin the *carapaus* and remove the centre bone. Close them again and put on a plate, side by side. Sprinkle lemon juice over the fish.

Mix oil, vinegar, salt and pepper and pour over the fish. Garnish with onion rings and small slices of garlic. Sprinkle with parsley.

Before serving, cover the plate with tin foil paper and keep in the refrigerator for a day or two.

In northern Europe it may be difficult to get fresh *carapaus* so here is an alternative version of this recipe:

Take the fish from four tins of pilchards (without bones or skin) and lay them carefully on a plate. Mix the remaining oil with vinegar, salt and pepper and pour over the sardines.
Sprinkle with small chopped onions, tomatoes and capsicum.

It is also possible to serve the sardines with an oil-egg-mustard sauce covered with onion rings and sprinkled with sweet paprika. Garnish with parsley and black olives.

Some of the fishermen in the Algarve specialise in catching only specific types of seafood. This is actually quite traditional and not only because of the hard economical situation. You may have noticed next to the beach near Burgau or Santa Luzia many earthenware pots with numbers on them. These are used to catch octopus.
The fishermen place hundreds of these pots without bait on the sea-bed in the shallow waters. Octopuses are drawn to these pots for the very simple reason that they like to lie in wait for their own prey in dark spots and caves. Sadly here too the catch has considerably decreased over the past years.

There are two ways to prepare octopus. The small ones do

not need to be tenderised, but the fishermen beat the large ones against rocks to soften them. Afterwards, the octopus is cooked in a pressure cooker and skinned.

An alternative way is to dry the octopus in the open air. Later they are grilled on charcoal, cut into small pieces and served.

The smell of grilled octopus is one of the most characteristic odours on feast days and holidays in the Algarve. Their tasty meat and strong flavour are very popular.

Here is a recipe for one of the specialities of the Algarve.

## OCTOPUS RICE *ARROZ DE POLVO*

| | |
|---|---|
| *1 kg octopus* | *1 glass red wine* |
| *1 cup oil* | *150 g onions* |
| *2 garlic cloves* | *350 g tomatoes* |
| *1 green capsicum* | *sprigs of parsley* |
| *piri-piri* | *salt* |

Clean the octopus thoroughly and wash in running water. Cut into small pieces. Finely chop the onion and garlic.

Pour boiling water over the tomatoes, skin them and remove the pips. Cut into small pieces.

Remove pips from capsicum and cut into small pieces.

Heat the oil and brown the onions and garlic, then add capsicum and tomatoes.

Add the octopus and cook for a few minutes. Add water

and wine and cook until tender.

   Season to taste with salt and piri-piri.

   Add rice and cook for a further 15 minutes.

   Sprinkle parsley on top and serve hot.


In the Algarve, lobster is caught throughout the summer months of May to September. Special baskets attached to long strings are lowered into the water with pieces of *peixe espada* as bait inside. Sometimes these baskets can be found on the beach as storm and rough seas easily break them off their attachments.

If you are interested in fishing there are two museums in Faro that portray the life of fishermen and their families in olden times: the Maritime Museum in the building that houses the Harbour Master (near the Praça D. Francisco Gomes), and the Ethnological Museum at the Praça da Liberdade at the far end of the pedestrian zone as seen from the harbour.


It is best to buy fresh fish in the Algarve from the fish markets where it is brought daily (except Sundays) directly from the fishing boats. At the fish stalls you can also buy another Algarvian speciality: *caracois* (snails). Those with particularly small shells are considered a delicacy and are scooped out with a tooth-pick.


The variety of fish and sea food in this part of the world is both wide and confusing. To familiarise yourself with a few names we have made the following list with the help of José Francisco Rodrigues Vieira, from Armação de Pera, who used to be a fisherman before he opened his restaurant.

This list is not complete of course. One can buy so many different types of fish between Vila Real de St. António and Sagres that they alone could fill an entire book.

**Ameijoas:** Clams.

There are very many different types of clam. A must for all *Caldeirada* dishes. In the Algarve clams can be bought throughout the year.

**Atum:** Tuna.

The best months for tuna are July and August when it is most likely to be caught off the Algarve coast.

**Berbigões:** Cockles.

Yellowish in colour and especially good with pork in *Caldeirada* dishes.

**Besugo**: Sunfish.

Appears in many different types and sizes. They are very tasty throughout the year and are best grilled.

**Cação:** Dogfish.

A species of shark, up to 2 metres in length, often used as an ingredient for *Caldeirada*.

**Camarão:** Prawns.

The word is used loosely in the Algarve in describing various types of prawns.

**Carapau:** Scad or Horse mackerel.

Similar in size and general appearance to sardines but with a lateral bony ridge.

**Cavala:** Mackerel.

Found all along the coast, weighs up to 1 kilogram, can be eaten throughout the year and is best grilled.

**Cherne:** Stone Bass.

A large fish and a favourite in the Algarve. It is cut into slices and grilled. It is also frequently boiled.

**Choco:** Cuttlefish.

Related to the squid (see *Lulas*) with a lot of black ink which may be retained to dramatic effect when serving grilled.

**Corvina:** Meagre.

A southern European fish which weigh as much as 40 kilograms. Tasty as cutlets.

**Dourada:** Gilt-head Bream.

Can be as heavy as 25 kilograms, but usually weighs only 1 to 5 kilograms. It is best when baked.

**Enguia:** Eel.

The eels in the Algarve can be as thin as a finger and taste delicious whichever way they are prepared.

**Espada:** Scabbard fish.

Usually a long and silvery fish, but can also be black. Very good for grilling.

**Espadarte:** Swordfish.

Can be as heavy as 250 kilograms and is therefore only sold in portions.

**Lavagante:** European lobster.
Blue-black with giant claws.

**Lagosta:** Rock or Spiny Lobster.
Lacks the big claws of its cousin, but just as tasty.

**Lagostim:** Dublin Bay prawns.
The largest of the prawn clan in the Algarve.

**Lampreia:** Lamprey.
Spawns in the rivers of northern Portugal. Looks and cooks like eels.

**Linguado:** Sole.
In the Algarve large sole is on offer for very reasonable prices even though they are often imported.

**Lingueirão:** Razor shells.
They live hidden in the sand and are favourites with rice dishes, such as *arroz de mariscos*.

**Lulas:** Squid.
When you buy them in the Algarve they are usually not gutted. The simplest preparation: Cut into rings and fry in oil or deep-fry.

**Mexilhões:** Mussels.
Clean, beard and cook lightly for a delicious starter.

**Moreia:** Moray eel.
Generally for sale is the so-called Mediterranean moray eel. Suitable for *caldeirada*.

**Ostra:** Oyster.
Portuguese oysters are highly recommended.

**Ouriço:** Sea urchin.

You should ask for them already gutted. The yellow ovaries are regarded in the Algarve a delicacy.

**Pargo:** Snapper

A white fleshed fish best grilled or baked in the oven.

**Peixe Galo:** John Dory

A 60 cm long, bony fish which tastes delightful. Availability very seasonal.

**Pescada:** Hake.

Restaurants may describe it, wrongly, as "whitefish" on their menus. Smaller hake is sometimes called *pescadinhas.*

**Polvo:** Octopus.

In the Algarve it is often cooked with rice. It is considered a delicacy by those who like it.

**Raia:** Skate.

Yet another suitable candidate for *Caldeirada.*

**Robalo:** Sea bass.

Can be up to 80 cm long and weigh 1 to 2 kilograms. An expensive, high quality fish that is best suited for grilling or frying.

**Rodovalho:** Turbot.

It is not often available in the fish markets. It is very good, but very expensive.

**Ruivo:** Gurnard.

Firm white flesh. Commonly served with boiled potatoes.

**Salmonete:** Red Mullet.

A delicately flavoured, but expensive fish which is best grilled.

**Santola:** Spider crab.

Easily identified by its spindly appearance and much appreciated in Portugal.

**Sapateira:** Common or Edible Crab.

The robust, oval-shelled fellow with big claws.

**Sardinhas:** Sardines.

Generally 15 to 20 cm length. Grilled or fried and best in the summer months.

**Solha:** Plaice.

Small plaice may be grilled whole. Otherwise fry or poach.

**Tamboril:** Monkfish.

Its very large head is an indispensable part of many fish soups.

**Tintureira:** Tiger Shark.

A member of the sand shark family. Can be as long as 1,5 metre. A *tintureira* caught in Sagres weighed over 100 kilograms, so the fishermen say.

**Truta:** Trout.

Surprisingly, trout is also a very tasty fish of this region. It comes straight from the rivers.

**Vieira:** Scallops.

The famous Coquilles St. Jacques are not very much in demand in the Algarve, but after many years of absence they have reappeared in the fish markets.

# Autumn

Autumn in the Algarve has its own special taste and smell.

It tastes of young wine that has only just matured in the cellars and is now ready to be drunk. It also tastes of all those delicacies sold in the *pastelarias,* pastry shops.

The first dry figs are being sold along with almonds, walnuts and peanuts.

The smell of hot *castanhas assadas* pervades the air. Here fresh chestnuts are roasted in salt unlike in northern Europe. The chestnut sellers prepare them in earthenware pots on small carts set up in the pedestrian zones of the Algarvian towns, waiting for hungry customers.

If farmhouse chimneys in the hills are smoking it is a sign that spirit is being distilled from figs, arbutus berries or even carobs.

The summer crowds have left the Algarve only to be replaced by long-term holidaymakers who like to spend the winter months here and for whom the Algarve has become a second home.

Autumn in the Algarve means harvest time of course. Now is the time to pick the oranges, the mandarins, the lemons and all those other citrus fruits, along with quince and pomegranate.

Formerly, autumn was the time for pig killing. This is not such a common event today although it does still take place in the less populated regions of the Algarve where folks still kill their pigs at home.

The killing of the pig means a feast day, a day when all family members, friends and relatives get together to talk, exchange news and above all eat and drink together.

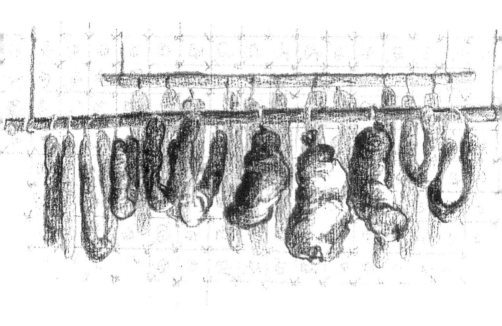

# KILLING
# THE PIG

It was sometime in November or December - certainly before Christmas - and the day for the kill had finally arrived. The pig had been well fed throughout the year and was sufficiently fat. Although opinions might have varied, it was generally thought that the moon was just right.

We are talking about times past, before the Algarve was overrun by today's crowds of tourists. It is still possible to see this once common annual event, but only in the remoter areas of the Algarve and only if you are fortunate enough to be specially invited.

The pig killing was a festive occasion with friends and relatives and neighbours who had come along to lend a helping hand. Even close acquaitances not seen for a long time would suddenly turn up for the occasion.

Seldom was the assistance of a professional butcher, a *matador*, required. Someone would usually know what to do.

The killing started early in the morning, early by Algarve standards that is. It would start with *filhós*, figs and *aguardente*. Everyone would stand in a circle, drinking and toasting each other with the words: *"para matar o bicho"* which roughly means "to kill the bugs."

After a few more glasses of *aguardente* and several more toasts to everyone's good health, the pig's time had come. This was a man's job. After the killing, the blood was drained and kept aside. The hair was singed with bushels of *erva com bicos* (grass with thorns) or *tojo* (prickly gorse). It was a man's task, too, to gut the pig.

The intestines, be used for sausages, were washed two or three times with soap and then with lemon juice, preferably in running water by a clean stream or river. A man's task again? No, this was the women's lot.

Whilst the women washed the intestines, the men cut the meat into portions, ably assisted by a generous intake of *aguardente*. Some of the blood (the remainder was later used for the blood sausages) was cooked with oil, onions, garlic, parsley, a few cloves, pepper, caraway seeds, salt and a little vinegar. Called simply *sangue de porco*, pork's blood, it was served with olives and bread. This would help to form a solid base to counteract the large quantities of alcohol being consumed.

The pig's liver was fried there and then along with all the other bits and pieces that could be used. If there was not sufficient to eat because too many people had arrived, one or two chickens were killed as well.

If you would like a recipe for the preparation of liver, here it is.

## PORK LIVER *FÍGADO DE PORCO*

| | |
|---|---|
| 500 g pork liver | 250 g onion rings |
| 1 cucumber | 250 g tomatoes |
| 1 tbsp vinegar | 1 garlic clove |
| 2 tbsp oil | 1 cup chopped parsley |
| salt, pepper | |

Cut liver into slices 2 cm long and fry in hot oil. Add chopped onions and garlic. Continue to fry.

Cut tomatoes and cucumber into cubes and add to the pan. Cover and simmer for 10 minutes.

Season to taste with salt, pepper and vinegar. Sprinkle with parsley.

Serve with hot potatoes.

Here is another very popular liver recipe that appears on the menus of many restaurants in the Algarve.

## MARINATED LIVER *ISCAS DE FÍGADO MARINADAS*

| | |
|---|---|
| *500 g pork liver (veal and beef liver are possible alternatives)* | *2 large onions* |
| | *1 bay leaf* |
| | *1/2 cup white wine* |
| *1/2 cup water* | *2 garlic cloves* |
| *salt, pepper* | *2 tbsp oil* |

Cut liver into thin slices and spread on a flat plate. Cut the onions and garlic into rings and spread across the liver.

Mix a marinade with wine, water, salt, pepper and oil. Pour over the liver, cover and stand for 2 to 3 hours.

Heat oil in a saucepan, dry the liver slices and fry in the hot oil. Add the onion rings and the marinade and stew.

Serve with potatoes or on toast.

The time is noon. The hard work has been done and by now everybody has changed from *aguardente* to wine.

The day the pig is killed is a day for getting together, for telling stories, talking about people, gossiping.

After the women have done the washing up, more bacon is thrown into a frying pan if there is not enough left over from all the previous frying. This is to produce the much loved crackling.

Crackling is a necessary ingredient for the sausages. Delicious small cakes are made from it as well.

## CRACKLING CAKES *COSTAS DE TORRESMOS*

| | |
|---|---|
| *1 lb ready-made bread or pizza dough* | *250 g crackling (from the butcher)* |
| *some flour* | |

Prepare the dough.

Heat the crackling in a pan and knead into the dough.

Spread the dough approximately 2 cm thick on to a wooden board sprinkled with flour. Shape into flat cakes about the size of your hand and place on a well greased tray.

Bake in a pre-heated oven of 150-180 degrees for 10 to 15 minutes.

If you cannot buy ready-made crackling, make your own with bacon. Cut into small cubes and brown in a pan.

We mentioned earlier that when the pig was killed its blood was carefully saved. In the Algarve it is the essential ingredient for sausages called *chouriço* or *chouriço preto*. In other regions of Portugal all sausages are called *chouriço* whether or not they are actually blood sausages.

## CHOURIÇOS

Streaky pork (belly pork for example) is passed through a meat grinder and mixed with a lot of crushed garlic and crackling.

Salt, ground pepper and pepper corn, a small amount of *massa de pimentos* (for preparation see page 61), caraway seeds, ground cloves, ground bay leaves, some red wine and a little bit of vinegar are mixed with the meat.

The blood is then added and stirred well before the intestines (sausage skins) are filled and then dipped briefly into boiling water.

The cooked *chouriços* are then smoked. Today, the traditional method of stringing up the sausages from wooden poles below the kitchen ceiling allows them to mature whilst food in the kitchen is being prepared over a wood fire.

Other Algarvian sausages, called *linguiças,* are also smoked in a similar way.

## LINGUIÇAS

Equal quantities of fat and lean pork are mixed together. One third of this mixture is cut into small cubes, the remaining two thirds are passed through a coarse meat grinder.

Crushed garlic is mixed with salt, ground pepper and pepper corns, a generous amount of *massa de pimentos* (for the colour of the sausages), bay leaves, cloves, and paprika.

This is then mixed well with the meat, covered and allowed to stand for any time between a few hours and a few days.

Before filling the intestines, the bay leaves, cloves and pepper corns are removed from the meat. They are then smoked without cooking first.

After they have matured, *chouriços* and *linguiças* can be grilled. The Algarvians have developed a technique using an earthenware mini-grill which cooks just one sausage at a time. The origin of these little gadgets goes back many years, but they have only recently been re-discovered and are now available in all souvenir shops.

To grill, the sausage has to be cut length wise and then opened up. The grilling bowl is filled with high-proof *bagaço* or *medronho* spirit. The sausage is put on the grill and the spirit lit. The result is indeed a delicacy

There is another speciality that we do not wish to keep from you called *paios de lombo*. The same spices are used as for *linguiças,* but the meat is fine pork fillet. Here is a recipe that allows you to prepare *paios de lombo* at home.

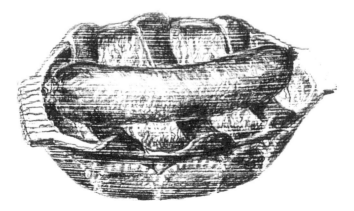

## PAIOS DE LOMBO

A pork fillet is cleaned of all fat and sinews. A spice mixture of salt, ground pepper and pepper corns, crushed garlic, cloves, bay leaves, *massa de pimentos*, ground paprika and some strong white wine is rubbed generously into the pork. The fillet is then covered and kept in the refrigerator for at least two days. Once in a while, the fillet is pierced with a little wooden stick.

Later the meat is dried and the cloves, bay leaves and pepper corns are removed.

The fillet is rolled tightly into netting and, just like a roast, tied with a string.

Hang up to smoke.

Should you not have suitable facilities to mature the sausages yourself, give the *paios de lombos* to someone who does have a wood fire or even a smoke chamber. They should not stay in the smoke as long as "ordinary" sausages.

There is a variation on *paios de lombos* called *paios brancos*. They are made the same way as *paios de lombos,* but instead of being smoked, they are dried in the air.

By the end of the pig killing day, the process of preserving the meat has been completed. If the meat has not been smoked it has been salted. As required for consumption throughout the year, it has been placed in wooden boxes or crates with alternate layers of salt. Bacon, ham, bones, ribs, the neck, the belly....

Afterwards? The night is still young. There are still many more stories to tell and much wine and *medronho* left.

Perhaps you would like to know what happened to the offal? Well, we managed to pick up a few basic recipes.

## LIVER, HEART & KIDNEYS WITH ONIONS *MOLEJA*

| | |
|---|---|
| 300 g pork heart | 300 g pork liver |
| 3 pork kidneys | 1/2 cup oil |
| 2 large onions | 1 tsp flour |
| 1 litre meat stock | 1/2 bay leaf |
| 3 garlic cloves | salt, pepper |
| 1 tbsp vinegar | |

Clean the kidneys. Throw the gristle away and cut into slices. Cut the heart into cubes and the liver into slices.

Heat the oil in a saucepan.

Start to brown the heart, then the kidneys and then the liver. Chop the onion and add to the meat.

Add the flour and mix thoroughly, then add the stock and the spices. Simmer for about 20 minutes.

Add vinegar to taste.

One can serve this dish with bread dumplings, but in Portugal one would probably eat it with boiled potatoes or noodles.

Offal can also be made into a soup, *Sopa de moleja*. You would only have to raise the amount of flour to 1 tbsp and the meat stock by an additional half litre.

# PORK BRAINS *MIOLOS DE PORCO*

| | |
|---|---|
| *250 g pork fillet* | *250 g pork brains* |
| *1 crushed garlic clove* | *1 tbsp lemon juice* |
| *1 tbsp oil* | *1 tbsp chopped parsley* |
| *2 eggs* | *2 tbsp bread crumbs* |
| *salt, pepper* | *oil to deep-fry* |

Cut the pork into slices one centimetre thick. Season with garlic, salt and pepper.

Stand for two hours.

Soak the brains in water, clean and skin. Mix brains, eggs, salt, lemon juice, bread crumbs and parsley.

Coat the pork slices with mixture and deep-fry in hot oil on both sides.

Serve with mixed salad.


Do not be put off by the sound of the next three recipes; they are delicacies. They are meals prepared with *testículos*, which the Algarvians call *alforges*.

If you like sweetbread or kidney then testicles may also be to your taste. Lamb testicles are the most popular in the Algarve, but calf's can be used too.

# TESTÍCULOS

| Recipe 1  2 onions | 500 g testicles |
|---|---|
| 2 garlic cloves | 2 cloves |
| 1/2 bay leaf | 1 tsp flour |
| 1/2 litre stock | 2 tbsp oil |
| salt, pepper | 1 tsp vinegar |

Soak the testicles in water. Cut into slices and fry in hot oil. Slice the onions, chop the garlic and add.

Follow with a sprinkling of flour and add stock. Cook for 5 to 8 minutes. Season to taste with vinegar.

| Recipe 2  1 egg | 500 g testicles |
|---|---|
| bread crumbs | salt, pepper, oil to fry |

Soak the testicles in water and cut into slices. Whisk the egg with salt and pepper and dip the testicle slices into the batter. Fry in hot oil and serve with salad.

| Recipe 3  2 tbsp oil | 500 g testicles |
|---|---|
| 1 tbsp lemon juice | 1 onion |
| salt, pepper, oil to fry | 2 tbsp flour |
| 1 cup ice cold water | some herb butter |

Wash and dry the testicles with a paper cloth. Cut into slices, 2 cm thick.

Prepare a marinade of oil, lemon juice, salt and pepper. Cut the onion in half and add to the marinade.

Put the testicles into marinade and stand for two hours. Remove the onion.

Mix flour with ice cold water and make into a dough. Cover the testicle slices with dough and deep-fry in hot oil. Cover with herb butter.


If we were to describe the following recipe in its original form, you would probably not want to prepare it, but as we have researched it we would like you to know about it at least.

*Cozido de milhos* is a stew based on corn that is eaten by the poor and rich alike on feast days such as weddings. Its preparation takes a long time and is bound to a strict tradition.

For example, the corn is cooked in ash, preferably fig wood. When it is soft after hours of cooking, the sprouts are removed by the women who combine this labour-intensive occupation with hours of gossip.

The ingredients include everything from the pig's head - ears and snout and other parts which some people consider delicacies.

The following recipe has been adapted to our taste and its preparation time has been made more realistic - hopefully without spoiling its original character.

## Corn Stew *Cozido de Milhos*

| | |
|---|---|
| 4 slices belly pork | 4 slices lean bacon |
| 2 small pig's trotters | 1 pork knuckle |
| 3 cloves | 1 carrot |
| 1 leek | 1 celeriac with leaves |
| 1 large onion | 1 tbsp oil |
| 1/2 tsp chopped basil | 1/2 tsp chopped thyme |
| 1/2 tsp caraway seeds | salt, pepper |

Soak trotters, knuckle and belly pork (ears too if you fancy them) overnight in very cold salt water.

To cook the meat, bring 1 1/2 litres of water with cloves, bay leaves, herbs and vegetables, salt and pepper to the boil. Put meat into boiling liquid and simmer until done.

Take the meat out of the broth and keep warm. Pass the broth through a fine sieve.

Add the corn to the broth and cook until tender. Season to taste.

Serve the corn on a plate and surround with meat, then cover with onion rings browned in oil.

## Stuffed Pig's Trotters *Pés Cheios de Porco*

| | |
|---|---|
| 4 pig's trotters | 1/2 litre water |
| salt, pepper | 1 tbsp oil |

| 1 egg | 1 tbsp chopped parsley |
| --- | --- |
| 1 tbsp chopped onion | 1 bread roll |
| 1 tbsp butter | 1 cup milk |

Put trotters into boiling salt water and cook until the skin separates. Take from the broth and while the trotters are still warm, carefully remove the bones without breaking the skin.

Tie one end of the skin with a cotton thread.

Fry the bread roll in butter and pour hot milk over it. Add onions, parsley and the egg. Season with salt and pepper.

With this mixture, fill the trotters and tie at the other end with cotton thread.

Fry on all sides in hot oil.

The stuffed pig's trotters taste very nice when they are hot and served with salad or vegetables. They are also rather good when cold and sliced.

# THE WINE OF THE ALGARVE

People who really understand wine and use knowledgable expressions such as "full-bodied," "fruity" and "noble" may not be terribly impressed by the wines of the Algarve. They do have a point, but not in every case.

It is fair to say that the wine you buy in the Algarve, not readily available elsewhere, does not usually generate cries of enthusiasm.

However, it is also true that the potential of Algarve wine has not been fully exploited.

Wine has been grown in the Algarve for hundreds of years, but the area only became an independent, demarcated wine-growing region comparatively recently.

The varieties of red grapes grown locally are Negra Mole, Periquita and Crato Preto. The white ones are mostly Crato Branco. Nearly all Algarve wines are a blend of different varieties of grape from different vineyards. The yield is of a good European average: approximately 3,000 to 4000 litres per hectare.

Climate and sandy ground give the grapes a high sugar content which in turn gives a high alcohol content of sometimes 14 percent.

Most of the wine is produced by four cooperatives which are located in Lagoa, Lagos, Portimão and Tavira. Only about 20 percent of all Algarve grapes are harvested and pressed by independent vintners today and much of that output is bottled by the cooperatives.

Virtually all the wine produced in the Algarve is table wine which is consumed while young and sold for prices that may hardly even cover the production costs. It is nearly all for domestic consumption; only 5 per cent is exported.

With the exception of a few aperitif wines, Algarve wine is rarely given much chance to mature. An exception is a white wine made from Crato Branco grapes called *Algarseco* produced by the Lagoa Cooperative. It is quite similar to Sherry and is produced by using the "Solera" method in which old wine is added to young. Unfortunately, the marketing is poor and, of course, what you don't know about, you don't buy.

This applies to a high proof spirit called *bagaço* which is distilled in Lagoa and is actually quite good. It is made from the residue of the white grapes and matures for at least five years in oak barrels which give it a brandy colour. It is an excellent drink, but when a bottle is on sale for under two pounds, the potential buyer may harbour some doubts as to its quality.

Although the climate is ideal for ripening grapes, there are still very many avenues to explore before there is any likelihood of discovering a really superior wine in the Algarve.

Nonetheless, if the Algarve wine does not please, the wine from the Alentejo is definitely worth trying. The prices are extraordinarily low and there is a wide variety of choice, including some very fine red wines indeed.

In summer, the light and slightly sparkling *vinho verde* from the north of Portugal is particularly refreshing. If you prefer dry white wines, you should try *Bucelas* from vineyards north of Lisbon and *Cartaxo* which is produced around a small town situated by the Tagus river.

A stay in Portugal is incomplete without tasting the most famous of all wines here: port wine. Port comes from the Douro valley and from the city of Oporto at the mouth of the river.

A long time ago, most of the wine from Portugal was exported to Great Britain but, it did not always travel well during long periods at sea. In order to maintain its sweetness and freshness, brandy was added. Port wine was born. It has not only retained its characteristic taste over the years, but has improved and grown to become one of Portugal's prime exports.

# AUTUMN MENU
# FROM THE DOM SEBASTIÃO RESTAURANT
# IN LAGOS

António Gomes had a dream: he wanted to open a restaurant offering Portuguese cuisine of a very high standard.

No paper napkins, only real cloth napkins. Costly crockery, candlelight and real flowers on the table, not plastic ones. There were to be specially selected wines, of course, and exceptional food.

Together with his Austrian wife, who attended a cookery college in Salzburg, António Gomes fulfilled this dream. In 1976 he opened the Dom Sebastião restaurant in Lagos and it continues to reflect his philosophy that for a quality restaurant only the very highest standards are acceptable.

If a restaurateur is able to sell more than 200 meals a day in a town like Lagos, which has fewer than 15,000 inhabitants but more than 250 eating establishments, he has 'arrived'. When regular clients return year after year to enjoy his food, one must say he is successful. There are, of course, reasons for this accomplishment.

António Gomes still personally goes to the market every morning to buy fresh fish. He never lets anyone else do it. He also does not believe in so-called seasonal price "adaptations" for tourists. Neither does he make concessions to foreign gastronomic preference or palate. A customer in his restaurant will enjoy the delights of Portuguese cuisine only.

For the autumn he has suggested a three course meal, starting with soup, followed by rice and seafood, with a caramel sweet as dessert.

## GARLIC SOUP *AÇORDA DE ALHO*

| | |
|---|---|
| *1 litre hot meat or vegetable stock* | *4 garlic cloves* |
| | *4 tbsp olive oil* |
| *4 eggs* | *2 tbsp chopped coriander* |
| *4 small slices old bread* | *salt, pepper* |

Use a mortar to make a paste of coriander, coarse sea salt,

olive oil and garlic.

Put this paste into four soup bowls, preferably earthenware, and top up with hot stock. Place bread slices on to the soup.

Poach the eggs for two minutes.

Carefully scoop out and position on top of bread slices.

In reproducing the following recipe for the main dish, it must be borne in mind that the ingredients are not always available and when they are, they are not necessarily cheap. Back home they may not be as fresh as when they are bought in the Algarve. We strongly recommend, therefore, you try the *Arroz de marisco* in the Dom Sebastião restaurant in Lagos. If you still want to try preparing the dish yourself, here's how.

## RICE WITH SEAFOOD *ARROZ DE MARISCO*

| | |
|---|---|
| *250 g razor clams* | *1/2 litre water* |
| *3 tbsp olive oil* | *2 cups chopped tomatoes* |
| *3 garlic cloves* | *1 tsp ground paprika* |
| *1 bay leaf* | *1 chopped onion* |
| *1/4 litre white wine* | *salt, pepper* |
| *500 g fish scraps (including a monkfish head)* | *200 g shrimps* |
| | *8 large prawns* |
| *12 mussels* | *150 g clams* |
| *2 crabs* | *1 small lobster* |
| *4 cups boiled rice* | *chopped, green coriander* |
| *1 tsp vinegar* | |

Boil the razor clams in 1/2 litre water until the meat can be separated from the shells. Save the water.

Heat oil in a large saucepan, add onions, garlic and tomatoes and fry until golden brown. Add water and white wine.

Season with salt, pepper, paprika and bay leaf.

Add the fish scraps, including the monk fish. Cover and cook for 20 minutes.

Pass the stock through a fine sieve, add the razor clam cooking water and cook slowly for a little longer.

Cut the clams into very small pieces and continue to cook in the stock. Then progressively add the pre-cooked lobster, the prawns and crabs and cook until done. Finally, add the thoroughly cleaned and well-soaked mussels.

Cook again for a further 10 minutes.

Take the seafood out of the liquid and arrange neatly on a plate. Serve the hot broth and the dry boiled rice, cooked in meat stock, in separate bowls.

Chop the coriander and serve individually with vinegar.


Coriander, explains António Gomes, appeals to the sense of smell, whereas a drop of vinegar provides the final touch for the perfect meal.

Although razor clams are a traditional ingredient of the *Arroz de marisco* they may not be easily available at home. As a substitute, we suggest you use ready-packed, pre-cooked crab meat.


There is pudding for dessert. António Gomes gave us his very own special recipe, handwritten, having found it after a lot of rummaging around in a drawer. *Pudim Molotov*, is available in many Portuguese restaurants, but we have not been able to find the origins of this dessert or why it is named after the famous Russian. One thing is clear: this is not a traditional Portuguese recipe although the ingredients are very familiar.

## MOLOTOV *PUDIM MOLOTOV*

| | |
|---|---|
| *10 egg white* | *200 g sugar* |
| *1 tsp lemon juice* | *2 tbsp water* |
| *2 cups ovos moles* | |

Whisk the egg white with half the sugar and the lemon juice to a very stiff consistency.

Mix sugar and water in a small pot and stir continuously until it has become caramel. Whisk the caramel into the beaten egg white.

Thoroughly grease an oven-proof dish and fill with the mixture.

Set into a bain-marie and cook in the oven at 150 degrees for approximately 20 minutes until of a stiff texture.

Stand to cool.

Prepare *ovos moles* with the egg yolk (see the recipe on page 26). Pour over the Molotov.

The preparation of *Pudim Molotov* is not easy. The most

critical moment seems to be when the caramel is mixed with the egg white. It is futile to give advice on this. One has to try it out.

What comes after the Molotov? To round off the meal in the Dom Sebastião there will be figs, almond liqueur, *medronho* or a clear fig *aguardente* from Tavira.

Sr. Gomes holds a remarkable collection of port wines, among which is a bottle of 1795 vintage. It is highly unlikely that he will open it.

# MEDRONHO,
# AGUARDENTE
# AND
# AMÊNDOA AMARGA

There is a spirit in the Algarve, pure and crystal clear, that the Algarvians, who still know how, distil in their own homes.

They drink it at every opportunity - on happy or sad occasions - with a little cup of strong black coffee, or after a meal to help digestion.

They call this *aguardente*. It is distilled from various things that exist in profusion in the Algarve, including the left-overs of the grapes after the wine pressing. This particular *aguardente* is called *bagaço* After it has been stored for some time, and if it has been distilled conscientiously, it is good enough to compete with any *grappa* or *marc*.

This is only one example of *aguardente*. There are many others. For example, *medronho*, a spirit made from the arbutus or strawberry bush. Some *medronho* is endowed with all the qualities of a superior fruit schnapps.

Distilleries in the Algarve, especially in the *serras*, are often in private hands. The required equipment can be bought easily. A still is called a *caldeira* and it is made from copper. Even those brands of *aguardente* marketed by well-known companies are quite often produced, not in large establishments, but in small privately-owned distilleries.

In the hills in particular, spirit is distilled by farmers and forestry workers. Every year they will regularly take a couple of weeks off to produce enough for themselves and their friends. Any surplus will be sold. This is not a strictly legal trade, but people here are not too finicky. A connoisseur will always prefer a privately distilled *aguardente* to that which has been produced commercially.

José da Silva Diogo owns a distillery between Olhão and Quelfes. He specialises in *aguardente de figo* (fig schnapps) and *aguardente de alfarroba* (schnapps made from the carob fruit).

*Figo aguardente* is made from windfalls. Although José Diogo has his own fig trees, he buys additional fruit. For seven or eight days the dried fruits are left in water to ferment. Then the distilling process begins. The addition of yeast is generally unnecessary.

Distilling is a simple chemical process: heating, evaporation and cooling down. The final result has an alcohol content of 40 to 42 percent and a taste that cannot be adequately described. *Aguardente de figo* must be tasted. Two hundred kilos of figs will produce up to 50 litres of *aguardente*.

There are no secret recipes and no additives. Nevertheless, generally the smaller the distillery, the better the *aguardente de figo*.

The distilling process for *medronho* is similar to the *aguardente de figo*. However, the wort is first fermented for 14 days and then it is kept in an airtight wooden barrel for a further two to four months prior to distillation.

Experts can judge the strength and quality of their product by filling a glass, shaking it and then watching the bubbles that

rise to the surface. Large bubbles that keep for a while are a sign of good quality. Another easy test is to rub a little *medronho* on to the back of your hand: it should not smell of figs. If it does, is not pure *medronho*. Like vodka and gin, practically all commercially and privately distilled *medronho* is colourless. If you come across a yellow-coloured *medronho,* you are fortunate. The yellow colour is gained from lengthy storage in oak barrels.

Farmers and forest labourers drink *medronho* and black coffee for breakfast. *Medronho* with honey from the hills is very good against colds. You can make cocktails by mixing one part *medronho* with three parts of honey melon juice and crushed ice, or equal parts of port wine and *medronho*.

José Diogo has two sites on which he distils 3,000 to 4,000 litres per year. He sells it to a manufacturer in Faro who sticks his own labels on the bottles, but José Diogo says the profit is so small that he has scarcely enough to pay a worker. He himself has now become a *solicitador*, a legal advisor.

In earlier times life was different. José Diogo had his own labels which he called "Dona Amélia" after his wife and "Maria Zizé" after his daughter. That was a long time ago and it was not very lucrative. Taxes, you understand....

In those days he used to produce *bagaço* as well as *genebra Portuguesa* (gin) and several liqueurs such as *amêndoa amarga*, an almond liqueur which exists in both sweet and bitter forms. Then there was *figomel*, an Algarve speciality made of honey and *aguardente de figo*; *rumel,* made of honey and rum, and *licor de leite,* a liqueur based on milk. We successfully persuaded Maria José to reveal the recipe for the last named.

# MILK LIQUEUR *LICOR DE LEITE*

The carob *aguardente* is especially suited, but any other clear spirit with no distinctive taste of its own will do.

| | |
|---|---|
| *1/2 litre aguardente* | *1/2 litre fresh milk* |
| *350 g sugar* | *1 vanilla stick* |
| *20 g cocoa* | *1 lemon* |

Cut the lemon into slices or, if you prefer, grate the lemon peel and squeeze some juice.

Mix the lemon slices, juice and other ingredients and put into a glass bottle or jar with a large opening.

Close tightly and stand for two to three weeks. Shake every other day.

Pour the liquid through a fine paper filter until it is clear. Fill a clean bottle and stand for a few more days.

# ORANGE LIQUEUR *LICOR DE LARANJA*

| | |
|---|---|
| *300 ml pure alcohol (90 percent)* | *peel of 3 oranges and 1 lemon* |
| *300 g sugar* | *300 ml water* |

The process for making orange liqueur is similar to that of

milk liqueur:

Cut the citrus peel into very small pieces and put with the other ingredients into a large glass bottle.

Shake thoroughly and close tight.

Stand the bottle for at least five days. Shake thoroughly at least twice a day.

Filter and fill into a new bottle.

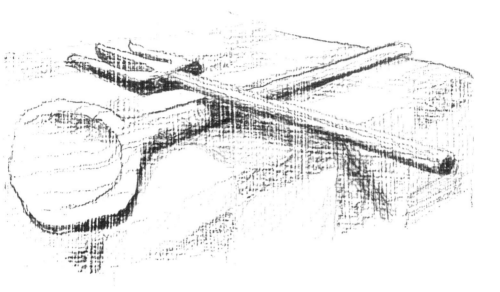

# AUTUMN
# RECIPES

The following recipes are not necessarily confined to the autumn season. They cannot really be categorised by season, so we have cheated a little and squeezed them in here because they are interesting and unusual.

One of the staple foods of the rural population in the Algarve has always been bread soup. It was eaten for breakfast at least once a week before work in the fields started. In view of the general economic situation it was a very sensible way of using left-overs.

## BREAD SOUP *AÇORDA DE PÃO*

| | |
|---|---|
| *1 1/2 litres vegetable, meat or fish stock* | *8 slices stale bread* |
| *1 garlic clove* | *4 tbsp olive oil* |
| *1 tbsp chopped parsley* | *4 eggs* |
| | *salt, pepper* |

Heat the olive oil in a saucepan.

Rub the garlic into the bread slices and fry on both sides in the hot oil.

Season the hot stock with salt and pepper. Whisk the eggs and fold into the hot stock.

Place two slices of the bread into each of the four soup plates and top up with soup.

Garnish with parsley.

*Portulak* has become quite rare in Britain as well as in the Algarve. It used to be a popular spice. However, it can still be found for sale in the better stocked vegetable shops and markets. If you cannot find *portulak* you will have to grow your own. Seeds are readily available.

## PORTULAK SOUP *SOPA DE BELDROEGAS*

| | |
|---|---|
| *500 g potatoes* | *1 bunch of Portulak* |

| | |
|---|---|
| 2 tomatoes | 1 onion |
| 2 garlic cloves | 2 carrots |
| 1 leek | 1 tbsp oil |
| 1 litre meat stock | salt, pepper |

Purée the vegetables in a blender or pass through a meat grinder.

Add the oil and stock and bring to the boil, then cook for approximately 10 to 15 minutes.

Season to taste with salt and pepper.

Chicken *piri-piri* (see page 61) is served in many Algarve restaurants, but especially those in the neighbourhoods of Monchique and Guia. Restaurants specialising in chicken *piri-piri* are usually brim full of Portuguese customers. Chicken in the Algarve really does taste delicious.

The following is a traditional recipe, which can be prepared with or without *piri-piri*.

## CHICKEN IN RED WINE *FRANGO BÊBADO*

| | |
|---|---|
| 1 chicken | 2 tbsp olive oil |
| 1 chopped onion | 2 crushed garlic cloves |
| 1 bay leaf | 2 cups chopped tomatoes |
| 1/4 litre red wine | 1 small glass bagaço |
| salt, pepper | |

Take a very fresh chicken and cut into four portions, then fry in hot oil. Add onions, tomatoes and garlic. Stew for approximately 5 minutes.

Season with salt, pepper and bay leaf. Add red wine. Cover and simmer for 20 to 30 minutes.

Pour a glass of *bagaço* over the chicken and serve with garlic bread and salad.

Images of the Algarve countryside inevitably include the shepherd with his dogs and his flock of sheep and goats. It is well known that mutton, lamb and kid here are of superb quality.

The next recipe is slightly different from the normal.

## LEG OF MUTTON IN THE POT *PERNA DE CARNEIRO NO TACHO*

| | |
|---|---|
| *1 leg of mutton, about 1.2 kg* | *1 garlic nodule* |
| *1 bunch of parsley* | *1 bay leaf* |
| *2 tbsp tomato paste* | *50 g butter* |
| *100 g pork lard* | *100 ml wine vinegar* |
| *250 ml dry white wine* | *100 ml water* |
| *pepper corns* | *4 cloves* |
| *800 g potatoes, cut into cubes* | *coarse (sea) salt* |

Clean the leg of mutton and remove all fat, sinews and skin.

Make a paste from the crushed garlic, some salt, oil and a little wine. Rub into the meat and stand for one hour.

Place the chopped parsley, bay leaf, cloves, quite a few pep-

130

per corns, vinegar, white wine, butter, lard and tomato paste into an earthenware pot and top up with 100 ml water. Stir well.

Place the meat into this marinade, cover and stand for two to three hours.

Stew the meat on a medium heat until done.

When the meat is cooked, add the potatoes and brown.

Serve the leg of mutton with potatoes and a mixed salad of tomatoes, capsicum, cucumbers and onions with a vinaigrette.

(Instead of leg of mutton, lamb or kid are pleasant substitutes).

Tripe is not an Algarve speciality. Nevertheless, good quality ready-cooked tripe can be found in most butchers and supermarkets.

We looked for and found a Portuguese tripe recipe. It was given to us by Teresa Carvalho from Viana do Castelo in the north of Portugal.

## TRIPE AND VEGETABLES *DOBRADA*

| | |
|---|---|
| *800 g tripe* | *1 leek* |
| *2 pieces of celery* | *1 tbsp tomato paste* |
| *1 clove* | *1/2 bay leaf* |
| *1 garlic clove* | *1 cup onion rings* |
| *1/2 cup oil* | *1/2 cup red wine* |
| *1/2 litre water* | *salt, pepper* |
| *parsley to garnish* | |

Cut the cooked tripe into very thin strips, 3 to 4 centimetres long.

Heat the oil in a saucepan and add the finely chopped leek, celery and crushed garlic. Cook until golden brown.

Add the onions, then the red wine and water.

Now put the clove, bay leaf, salt, pepper and tripe into the boiling liquid. Simmer on a low heat until done.

Turn into a thicker consistency by adding the tomato paste.

Season to taste and sprinkle with parsley.

Serve with boiled potatoes.

Because of the Algarve's special climate, potatoes can be harvested several times during the year. Even in the autumn, "new" potatoes are available in the markets. The reddish varieties are especially tasty and at their best when not too large.

## POTATO STEW *COZINHADO DE BATATAS*

| | |
|---|---|
| *500 g potatoes* | *250 g sweet potatoes* |
| *1 tbsp flour* | *2 tbsp oil* |
| *1 clove* | *1/2 bay leaf* |
| *1 tsp vinegar* | *salt, pepper* |
| *1 onion* | *3/4 litre water or stock* |

Peel the potatoes and cut into thin slices.

Brown the flour with 1 tbsp oil and add the water or stock.

Season with salt, pepper and bay leaf. Cook for 5 minutes.

Add the potato slices and cook until soft. Keep stirring. Season with pepper and vinegar.

Cut the onion into slices, brown in oil and cover it with the potatoes.

Should you not wish to be totally without meat, you can add a small sliced liver sausage, or Portuguese *chouriço* or *linguiça* to the potatoes while they cook.

## CORNMEAL WITH SARDINES
### *PAPAS DE MILHO COM SARDINHAS*

| | |
|---|---|
| *20 sardines* | *200 g corn flour* |
| *1 litre meat stock* | *2 chopped tomatoes,* |
| *1 tbsp chopped onion* | *without skin or pips* |
| *1 tbsp chopped parsley* | *1 tbsp vinegar* |
| *2 tbsp oil* | *salt, pepper* |

Gut and clean the sardines and cut off their heads.

Place the fish into boiling salt water for 2 minutes, then remove the skin.

Heat the onion and tomatoes in oil until brown. Add stock, season to taste with salt and pepper, and bring to the boil.

Add the corn flour and mix into a porridge-like consistency.

Continue to stir until the porridge lifts itself from the bottom of the pot.

134

Surround with sardines on a plate, sprinkle with parsley and serve with green lettuce.

(There is a detailed description of *papas* and a basic recipe with further variations on page 39)

## DREAMS SONHOS

| | |
|---|---|
| *1 cup flour* | *1 cup cold water* |
| *1 tbsp oil* | *1 tbsp sugar* |
| *1 tsp baking powder* | *3 eggs* |
| *sugar and cinnamon to sprinkle* | *oil to fry* |

Mix the flour with the water and add the oil. Stir and cook until the mixture rises from the bottom of the pot. Remove from the heat.

Step-by-step, add eggs, sugar and baking powder and whisk until smooth.

Scoop this mixture in teaspoon-size dollops and bake in hot oil. Sprinkle with cinnamon and sugar.

*Sonhos* are excellent on their own, but can be served with the following sauce:

| | |
|---|---|
| *200 g sugar* | *1 tbsp ground orange peel* |
| *1 cup orange juice* | *1 cup port wine* |
| *1 tbsp honey* | *1/2 tsp ground cinnamon* |

Cook the sugar with the orange peel and juice into a thick consistency. Add the honey and cinnamon.

Take off the heat and add the port wine.

Serve the sauce hot or cold with the *sonhos*.

## SWEET FLOUR SOUP *CALDO DE FARINHA*

| | |
|---|---|
| 1 cup flour | 3 tbsp sugar |
| 1/2 tsp ground cinnamon | 1 tbsp ground lemon peel |
| 1/2 litre water | 1/2 litre milk or fruit juice |

Brown the flour in a saucepan and add the water. Continue to stir and add sugar, cinnamon and lemon peel. Cook for 5 minutes.

Add milk or fruit juice. The soup can be enhanced with finely chopped fresh fruit.

## ROYAL CAKE *BOLO REAL*

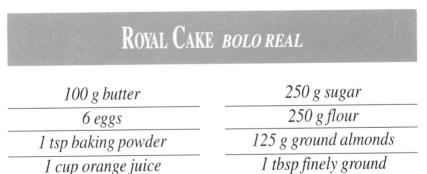

| | |
|---|---|
| 100 g butter | 250 g sugar |
| 6 eggs | 250 g flour |
| 1 tsp baking powder | 125 g ground almonds |
| 1 cup orange juice | 1 tbsp finely ground |
| 1 cup doce de chila | orange peel |

Separate the eggs. Whisk sugar and butter until frothy.

Continue to stir and gradually add the egg yolk, the flour mixed with baking powder and the ground almonds.

Whisk the egg white and carefully fold into the texture. Add orange peel and juice and stir until creamy.

Fill half the mixture into a well-greased baking tin and cover with *doce de chila*. Then cover with remaining dough and bake in a pre-heated oven at 200 degrees for approximately 50 minutes.

(Vanilla caramel can be used instead of *doce de chila*).

Winter

In the Algarve, winter is not really winter as northern Europeans know it. It is not a time of passing, but rather when time stands still.

At noon the sun is low but still warm and the temperature is as mild as any north European spring. The Algarve climate is the mildest in Portugal.

Flowers, trees and shrubs take their turn to come into bloom. The orange harvest is at its peak, yet the countryside is still somewhat subdued because Nature has not yet presented itself in all its full luxuriance

The Algarvians may experience *saudades*, a difficult word to translate which alludes to a feeling of loneliness, solitude, melancholy and self-pity. Happily, this feeling does not last for too long.

Although the climate is generally mild, storms sometimes blow in from the sea and there are rainy days, far too few for this region some years. Rain and wind both clear the mind.

Winter, like winter in northern Europe, is also a festive season of family get-togethers involving as many relations as possible. It is the season to share extended meals that may last for a whole day. Friends and relatives visit each other. The hospitality in the Algarve is always warm and guests are plied with traditional dishes, cakes, figs, olives and almonds.

In winter, too, the Algarvians start work again in the fields. After the rain has soaked the ground, they can be seen ploughing with their oxen or mules as they have done for hundreds of years. *Favas*, *ervilhas* and *grãos* are sown. Also in winter, the Algarvians cut their vines.

# FRUITS
## OF THE ALGARVE

The following story is probably more of a fairy tale or a legend and may not have happened at all, but it is well known and can be read in every tourist guide. As it is a lovely story, we want to re-tell it here.

Once upon a time there was a prince from the Orient who lived somewhere between Sagres and Tavira when the Moors ruled the Algarve. This prince fell in love with a princess who came from the far north of Europe

Suddenly one winter the princess became very ill. She was homesick for the snow of her homeland. She fell ill again the following winter and came close to death, so the prince planted a forest of almond trees around the palace.

Another year passed and in February doctors gave the princess only a few days to live. But the prince carried his beloved in his arms to the window of his palace. Who could describe her surprise when she looked out at a sea of almond blossom as white as the snow of her homeland.

Together they lived happily for many more years. The princess had her snow and the Algarve had one of its most prominent fruits - the almond.

*Massa de doce regional* is made from almonds. This is the famous marzipan used by Algarvian women to create the most delicious sweets (see page 152).

Almonds are the base and filling for many cakes and sweets, two of which we would like to introduce to you.

## CARRASQUINHAS

| | |
|---|---|
| *250 g almonds* | *250 g sugar* |
| *2 tbsp lemon juice* | *2 egg whites* |

Blanch the almonds, remove the skin and cut into very fine, thin slices. This is achieved quite successfully when the almonds are still moist.

Whisk the egg white, sugar and lemon juice to a very stiff consistency. Gently fold the almonds into it.

Use a teaspoon to position small portions on to a well greased baking tray.

Place the tray into the still cold oven. Dry rather than bake at a very low temperature for approximately 20 to 30 minutes.

If preferred, a small blob of *ovos moles* (see page 26) can be added to the *carrasquinhas*.

## FALSE FIGS *FIGOS DE AMÊNDOA E CHOCOLATE*

| | |
|---|---|
| *250 g sugar* | *250 g ground almonds* |
| *1 egg* | *1 tbsp ground candied* |
| *1 tbsp cocoa* | *lemon peel* |
| *1 tbsp ground candied* | *1 tbsp double cream* |
| *orange peel* | *1 tbsp milk* |
| *1 tsp vanilla sugar* | *1 cup water* |
| *2 tbsp sugar to sprinkle* | |

Boil sugar and water for approximately five minutes.

Add the almonds, milk, cream and vanilla sugar and set aside. Stand to cool.

Whisk the egg and fold into the mixture.

Add the cocoa, orange and lemon peel and knead into a dough. Mould into fig-like shapes and sprinkle with sugar.

Cool in the refrigerator for 1 to 2 hours.

From false figs to the real ones.... Figs grow on trees that shape the image of the Algarve as much as the almond trees do. They are short trees with wide branches and sometimes a quite bizarre appearance. For over 2,000 years, fig trees have been a symbol of fertility and well-being in all southern European countries.

Fig trees are complicated plants. They belong to the same family as the mulberry tree and have a complex love life. Figs only become edible when their tiny female flowers are pollinated by a certain species of bee.

There are dark blue and sometimes aubergine-coloured figs, green and yellow ones in numerous varieties. They have names such as *castelhano, rinho, coito* or *São Luís*. They all have their own taste but only experts can distinguish one from another.

Fresh figs, reputedly a laxative, contain many minerals such as phosphorus and calcium. Dry figs have a lot of iron.

Figs can be converted into alcohol, wine or a coffee substitute. Above all in the Algarve they are eaten fresh when available, dry out of season, on any occasion and at any time of the day. As well as being refreshing, they are very filling.

The main harvest season is June/July and September. Before the fruit is collected, farmers clean the grass around the trees. Windfalls are used as fodder for pigs or taken to be distilled into *aguardente de figo*.

The process of drying figs is rather elaborate. One has to accurately judge when the fruit can be picked for it is liable to attack by worms or insects. Once picked, the figs are spread on mats. These mats used to be made from very thin fennel twigs and are quite similar to bamboo canes. A few farmers still use them today, but most work with reeds which are also like bamboo. When there is a change of weather, the mats are simply rolled up and set aside with the figs still inside.

Dry figs by custom are stored in small baskets lined with paper. They are placed in layers with small twigs of the pepper bush called *daro*, an Arabic word. Seeds of wild fennel (*funcho*) and sometimes thyme, cinnamon or aniseed are added. Everybody seems to have their own recipes. The pepper or mastic bush that grows wild in the Algarve fields contains tannic acid and resin. Fennel has a special aroma and is supposed to keep insects at bay. In the end, the baskets are closed well to keep the figs from drying out completely.

Figs may also be dried by roasting them in the oven. They are then called *torrados*. Roasting creates a distinctive and fruity taste unknown to us at home.

Figs taste best of all fresh from the tree and as such are most suitable for a delicious fruit stew.

## Stewed Figs *DOCE DE FIGOS*

| | |
|---|---|
| *3 figs per person* | *1 glass Madeira wine* |
| *1 tbsp honey* | |

Wash the figs and gently pierce with a fork. Place them into a small pot on top of each other.

Mix the Madeira wine and honey, and pour over the figs. Cover and stand for an hour.

Then, still covered, simmer on a low heat for approximately 10 minutes. Serve lukewarm.

They taste particularly good with vanilla custard.

The Algarvians also like to flambé their figs with *aguardente de figo*.

Visitors who come in the autumn may notice numerous quince trees. Sadly, most of them are not, and will not, be harvested. There are several reasons for this. One of the main explanations is the fact that very few people seem to know what to do with them. One possible use ought to be obvious. After all, the word "marmalade" is derived from the Portuguese *marmelo*, meaning quince.

## QUINCE JELLY *GELEIA DE MARMELO*

| | |
|---|---|
| *1 litre quince juice* | *500 g preserving sugar* |
| *2 schnapps glasses of Calvados* | *rum or brandy* |

Rub the quince skin clean, wash and cut into small pieces.

Place quince into approximately two litres of cold water and simmer slowly to extract the juice.

Pass the pulp through a fine sieve. Boil the juice with the sugar and add the Calvados.

Just before the liquid turns into jelly, pour into jars.

Seal the jars when the jelly is still hot.

## QUINCES IN RED WINE *MARMELOS EM VINHO TINTO*

| | |
|---|---|
| *4 quinces* | *2 cloves* |
| *1 tbsp honey* | *1 cinnamon stick* |
| *1 cup of sugar* | *1/2 litre red wine* |
| *125 ml orange juice* | *1 tbsp raisins* |

Peel the quince and scoop out the pips with a knife.

Bring the red wine, the orange juice, sugar, honey and spices to the boil and set aside.

Place the quinces side by side in a saucepan and pour the liquid over them. Simmer on a low heat until the quinces are cooked.

Put the quinces into a bowl.

Pass the red wine sauce through a fine sieve, add the raisins and continue to cook until the liquid is reduced by half.

Now fill the quinces with the raisins, pour sauce over them and serve hot.

The next recipe follows on from the previous one. Additionally, icing sugar and some dough are required. Although it may not be typical of the Algarve, we recommend you use puff pastry.

Having cooked as above, take the quinces out of the stock and dry.

Take four pieces of squarely cut puff pastry and position the quinces in the centre. Fold the dough above the quinces (just like folding a sweet into a piece of paper).

Place on a well-greased baking tray. Bake in a pre-heated oven of 200 degrees for approximately 20 to 25 minutes until golden brown. Sprinkle with icing sugar.

As before, pass the red wine sauce through a fine sieve and cook to reduce quantity. Season with a glass of Madeira and serve hot with the quince pastries.

Many well-known fruits are grown in the Algarve, such as apples, pears, grapes - and strawberries which really taste of strawberries and can be bought, weather permitting, as early as January or February every year. There are peaches and apricots, chestnuts, walnuts and peanuts.

There are also several fruits that grow here but are relatively unknown to us, for example the pomegranate and the loquat.

*Reneclaudes*, cultivated sweet plum, are used by the people in Monchique to make their *Ameixada*.

## STEWED PLUMS *AMEIXADA*

| | |
|---|---|
| 1 kg wild plums without stones | 1 cup of sugar |
| 1 vanilla pod or | 1 tsp vanilla sugar |
| 2 cinnamon sticks or | 1 tsp ground cinnamon |
| 2 tbsp rum | 1 cup plum or fruit juice |

Bring the juice with sugar, vanilla and cinnamon to the boil.

Add the plums and cook on a low heat by stirring continuously until they are soft.

Remove the vanilla and cinnamon sticks.

Season to taste with rum and stand to cool.

Did we forget any fruits? Of course we did! The citrus fruits! Lemons, various kinds of mandarins, tangerines, clementines and other types of oranges.

Citrus trees have long been cultivated in the Algarve but not until a few decades ago were they planted in quantity. Inevitable progress in mechanisation and modern irrigation techniques have considerably accelerated the development and propagation of different varieties of citrus trees.

Oranges, lemons and grapefruit need careful soil preparation and cultivation, and much more water than indigenous fruits. However, they are less labour-intensive to grow and bring much more profit than almonds, olives, carobs, figs and grapes. Citrus fruits have become the main crop of the Algarve.

What could be more enjoyable than buying fruit in the middle of winter, fresh from the tree, at ridiculously low prices? Fruit that has ripened, not artificially, but naturally. Is there anything more delightful than seeing and smelling blossom and fruit on the same tree, in spring?

Although the majority of oranges ripen in the winter, they can be harvested throughout the entire year. As long as they are not picked, they keep well on the tree for a remarkably long time. What is to be done with them?

Of course, one must eat them and drink their fresh juice. What else? The Algarvians produce a light orange liqueur that is not unlike Cointreau.

Why not try to make marmalade with the oranges? It will cost you a fraction of what you will have to pay in the supermarket.

## ORANGE MARMALADE *CITRINADA DE LARANJA*

| | |
|---|---|
| *1 litre fresh orange juice* | *500 g preserving sugar* |
| *2 small glasses Cointreau* | *1 orange peel* |
| *1 tbsp lemon juice* | |

Press oranges to make the juice. Take one orange, separate the peel and cut into very thin strips. Do not keep the white inner skin; use only the orange coloured exterior rind.

Bring the rind, orange and lemon juice to the boil and add the sugar.

Boil for 4 to 5 minutes.

Add the liqueur.

Just before the liquid starts to gel, fill into glass jars and close tightly.

# SWEET SECRETS FROM THE PASTELARIA ALMEIDA IN PORTIMÃO

For more than 60 years she has been sitting at her marble table among colours, little pieces of wood and scented dough. Her nimble, agile fingers produce the most delightful creations: tiny fruits and animals made from marzipan known in the Algarve as *massa de doce regional.*

Maria de Lourdes Almeida Dias is now in her eighties. She is a tiny, fragile lady who openly displays the joy and pleasure it gives her to have such a creative occupation, even after so many years.

Her marble table is situated in the Almeida pastry shop at Largo 1º de Dezembro in Portimão. Her father founded the shop and since then sweets have been produced here for which the Algarve has become famous. They are made with fruits of the region - figs and almonds - and with sugar and eggs.

This delightful confectionary is sold to both Algarvians and to tourists. The little tea-shop in front of the working rooms has only recently been set up, probably under the influence of Maria de Lourdes' successor, her daughter Maria da Conceição. One day she will take over the business - her mother's hands don't work quite as well as they used to.

We watched Maria de Lourdes at her work and asked her and her daughter for the recipes for their sweets. They did not tell us everything, but they did tell us a little.

The main component is marzipan. In ordinary cookery books the general recommendation is to use icing sugar and egg white as ingredients for marzipan. But things are different in the Pastelaria Almeida. Even aromatic additions such as rose oil are omitted.

Why does this marzipan still taste so delicious? Probably because of the quality of the ingredients, particularly the almonds.

## MARZIPAN *MASSA DE DOCE REGIONAL*

| *250 g almonds* | *250 g sugar* |
| --- | --- |
| *1 cup water* | |

Blanch the almonds with boiling water and remove the skin. Carefully dry in the sun or a warm oven.

Pass the almonds through a meat grinder or through an electric blender until they have become as fine as flour.

Cook the sugar in the water until it is reduced to one third of its original quantity. The sugar must not be allowed to brown!

Knead the sugar syrup and almond flour into a dough until it is workable. Continue to knead.


At this point Maria de Lourdes takes the marzipan and forms mostly fruit shapes, but also animals such as fish or little figures. She uses small pieces of wood, particularly when she wants to create a fish with scales or a lemon with porous skin.

The marzipan mixture can also be tinted. For this Maria de Lourdes likes to use imported colours. Sometimes she fills her little works of art with *fios de ovos* or *ovos moles*. It is of utmost importance for her to use only fresh ingredients and to use them right away. Marzipan cannot be kept for long. Once it is dry it will lose its taste.

Marzipan is only a small part of the general output of the Pastelaria Almeida. There is also, for example, *nogado Algarvio* which is not a nougat but cracknel and one of the Almeida's spe cialities.

## CRACKNEL *NOGADO ALGARVIO*

| | |
|---|---|
| *500 g sugar* | *500 g peeled almonds,* |
| *1 tbsp vanilla sugar* | *coarsely chopped* |
| *(or some vanilla essence)* | *1 tbsp honey* |

Mix sugar and vanilla, and brown in a saucepan. Stir continuously while doing so. Add honey and almonds.

Spread some oil on a marble or stone plate.

When the mixture becomes liquid, pour instantly on the stone plate and use a knife to spread flat and evenly. This will determine the thickness of the *nogados*.

Cut into strips and allow to cool.

If preferred, wait for it to cool and then break it into pieces.

Another special delicacy on offer at Pastelaria Almeida is *Bolos Dom Rodrigo*.

It is not clear why these cakes were so named. Maybe they were named after Roderich, the last king of the Visigoths.

The way Maria de Lourdes makes *Bolos Dom Rodrigo* is unique. It is quite understandable, therefore, that we could not extract from her all the secrets of their preparation. But one thing she did tell us is that she only uses fresh eggs from free-range chickens, not the mass-produced ones.

## DOM RODRIGO'S SWEETS BOLOS DOM RODRIGO

| | |
|---|---|
| *2 cups fios de ovos* | *1 cup of sugar* |
| *150 g skinned and finely ground almonds* | *1/2 cup water* |
| | *1 glass advocaat* |
| *1 glass aguardente* | *6 egg yolk* |
| *some flour* | *3 tbsp sugar* |
| *1 tsp cinnamon* | |

Soak the *fios de ovos* (see page 25) in *aguardente*.

Cover a tray with some flour and place small portions of *fios de ovos* on it. Make a small indentation in the centre of the *fios de ovos*.

Bring sugar and water to the boil and cook for 5 minutes.

Add the almonds, stir well and set aside.

Whisk the egg yolk with the advocaat and gently fold into the mixture. Cool.

Take a teaspoon of the almond egg mixture and fill the *fios de ovos* nests. Sprinkle with sugar, cinnamon and some caramel sugar.

There is an alternative....

Mix sugar and cinnamon in a small saucepan and stir until very brown.

When the texture becomes liquid use a teaspoon to fill the *fios de ovos* nests with this sugary syrup.

Stand in the refrigerator for 2 to 3 hours.

These ingredients should be sufficient for approximately 15 to 18 little *Bolos Dom Rodrigo*.

They should not be too hard. That is why the Pastelaria Almeida sells them in silver tinfoil paper. Other places sell them in colourful wrappers.

And so to a few more recipes from the Pastelaria Almeida in Portimão....

## *MORGADINHOS DE AMÊNDOA*

Tiny, sweet-sized cakes are made of an almond-sugar mixture like marzipan, although the ground almonds can be a little more coarse. They can then be filled with *ovos moles*, *doce de chila* and *fios de ovos*.

Cover a baking tray with some flour and brown the cakes in the oven. Coat with icing sugar.

## CROQUETES

| | |
|---|---|
| *250 g figs* | *200 g chopped almonds* |
| *50 g cocoa* | *100 g sugar* |
| *1 dash of aguardente* | *sugar to coat* |

Pass the figs through a meat grinder.

Mix almonds, figs and all other ingredients in a saucepan and stir on a low heat until the texture has become hard.

Cool.

Shape into little sticks or sausages. Coat with sugar.

## FIG STARS *ESTRELAS DE FIGOS*

Flatten the dry figs.

Insert skinned and halved almonds into the outer edge of the fruit to create a star-like pattern.

Place on a baking tray dusted with flour. Heat in the oven until the almond tips have become brown.

## STUFFED FIGS *FIGOS RECHEADOS*

Gently remove the flesh from the inside of the dry figs. Take care not to damage the skin!

Make a mixture of sugar, almonds and figs as described for the croquetes above and stuff the figs with it.

The stuffed figs are wrapped in white paper, the ends of which are twisted like sweets. They are tied together just like garlic or onions.

The following recipe has been adapted for preparation at home. Algarve women will not use butter milk or baking powder but have their own raising agents.

## ALMOND SLICES *FATIAS DE AMÊNDOA*

| (for the dough) | 2 cups of sugar |
|---|---|
| 4 cups of flour | 2 cups butter milk |
| 1 1/2 packets of baking powder | 1 vanilla pod |
| (for the cover) | 200 g finely sliced almonds, without skin |
| 2 cups double cream | |
| vanilla sugar (or vanilla stick) | 1 cup sugar |
| | icing sugar to sprinkle |

Pass the flour with the baking powder through a sieve and mix with vanilla and butter milk.

Spread thinly on a baking tray.

Mix the almonds with cream, sugar and vanilla. Spread evenly on the dough.

Bake in a pre-heated oven of approximately 180 degrees for 45 minutes.

Cut into strips and sprinkle with icing sugar.

We would love to continue talking about *ovos moles* coated with icing sugar, or about *rebuçado de ovos*, a filling of *ovos moles* with almonds, or even about *doce de amêndoa* and many more sweetmeats. But here we must draw to a close. If we have whetted your taste buds, you may want to find time to pay a visit to Maria de Lourdes and her daughter in the tea and pastry shop at Largo 1° de Dezembro in Portimão.

# WINTER
# RECIPES

Winter time is cabbage time. Cabbage time? In Portugal, cabbage is an important food item and it comes as red cabbage, white cabbage, chinese cabbage, savoy cabbage, cauliflower or curly kale. All are cultivated in the Algarve.

"Cabbage warms the body," according to the Algarvians. Despite the generally warm climate, evenings and nights here can often be cold, so warming the body is often necessary.

*Caldo verde*, probably Portugal's most famous soup, is made from cabbage and potatoes. There are several recipes for it, but they are all quite similar. It is not originally an Algarvian speciality, but you will find it on just about every menu in every restaurant in the province. We have included it in this cookery book so that you will know what you are eating.

Opinions vary, but we incline towards recipes for *caldo verde* in which potatoes rather than cabbage predominate.

## SHREDDED CABBAGE SOUP *CALDO VERDE*

| | |
|---|---|
| *500 g finely chopped kale* | *500 g peeled, chopped potatoes* |
| *2 chopped garlic cloves* | |
| *1 chopped onion* | *1 litre meat stock* |
| *1 cup oil* | *1/4 litre cream* |
| *1 cup roasted white bread cubes* | *salt* |
| | *pepper* |

Heat the oil in a saucepan and add the onions and garlic. Cook until golden brown.

Add the kale and allow to "shrink," then add the stock.

Add the potatoes and cook for 20 to 30 minutes until they are soft.

Mash the potatoes in the broth to a creamy consistency.

Add salt and pepper to taste, followed by the cream. Garnish with roasted bread cubes.

Roasted onion rings or chopped hard-boiled eggs could be an alternative garnish.

# CABBAGE STEW *COZIDO ALGARVIO*

| | |
|---|---|
| *500 g coarsely chopped curly kale* | *250 g peeled and chopped potatoes* |
| *200 g red beans* | *1 litre meat stock* |
| *2 tbsp lard* | *1 chopped onion* |
| *1 chopped garlic clove* | *150 g linguiça (or garlic sausage)* |
| *150 g chouriço (or blood sausage)* | *2 slices lean, smoked bacon* |
| *4 spare ribs (approx. 1 kg)* | *2 tbsp olive oil* |
| *1 garlic clove* | *4 slices of bread* |
| *salt, pepper* | |

Heat the lard in a saucepan on a very hot stove and add the potatoes; cover.

Ten minutes later, add the onions, and when the potatoes form a crust at the base of the pot add the kale. Stir well.

Pour 1/4 litre of meat stock over it, cover and simmer until done.

Season to taste with salt and pepper.

Soak the beans in water overnight.

Bring beans and garlic in the remaining meat stock to the boil.

After the beans have cooked for 15 minutes, add the ribs, the lean bacon, the *linguiça*, and *chouriço*. Season with salt and pepper and cook until tender, but not too soft.

Rub garlic into the bread slices and fry in hot oil.

Arrange the vegetables on a plate and surround with the meat, cutting the sausages into slices.

Season the bean broth and serve separately.

Place bread slices into individual bowls, then fill with vegetables and meat. If preferred, top up with broth.

The meal improves greatly if it is prepared the previous day and then reheated. In this case, the meat ought to cook separately in broth.

A final tip for the *Cozido Algarvio*: It is possible (some recipes insist on it) to use white cabbage or chinese cabbage instead of kale.

## CABBAGE WITH MINCED MEAT *COZIDO DE REPOLHO*

| | |
|---|---|
| *1 kg white or chinese cabbage* | *250 g potatoes* |
| *250 g minced meat* *(half beef/pork)* | *1 onion* |
| | *1 tsp caraway seeds* |
| *1 tsp oil* | *2 cups meat stock* |
| *1 tsp chopped parsley* | *salt, pepper* |

Heat the oil in a saucepan. Add the onion and minced meat and fry on a high heat. Add the meat stock.

Cut potatoes into small cubes and cut cabbage into thin strips. Add to the stock.

Sprinkle the caraway seeds on top and season with salt.

Cover and stew, stirring intermittently.

Season to taste with pepper and garnish with parsley.

Sometimes in winter there may not be that many leaf vegetables available and so the Algarvians then eat a lot of pulses. These are available in great variety and quantity in all the markets.

## BEAN STEW  *FEIJOADA ALGARVIA*

| | |
|---|---|
| *300 g red or brown beans (other recipes recommend white beans)* | *3 slices belly pork* |
| | *100 g linguiça (or garlic sausage)* |
| *1 onion* | *2 garlic cloves* |
| *1 tomato* | *1 tbsp oil* |
| *1 1/2 litre water* | *2 tbsp chopped parsley* |
| *salt, pepper* | |

Cook the beans in the water until they are soft.

Cut the meat, onions, tomatoes and garlic into cubes and fry in very hot oil. Add to the beans.

Cut the sausage into slices and add to the mixture.

Continue to simmer for a further five minutes or until done.

Season to taste with salt and pepper and sprinkle with parsley.

And so to *bacalhau,* one of Portugal's best-loved foods and a subject of never ending discussion. To start with, what is this *bacalhau* that everybody talks about? Actually, it's only dried cod.

It was in the 16th century that Portuguese seamen first brought *bacalhau* back home. Cod is not found around the shores of Portugal. It used to be caught exclusively in the waters off Newfoundland, but nowadays it is also caught in the seas near Spitsbergen. It is landed on Portugal's west coast and dried on low wooden bars in the sun. Salted, it will last for half a year.

It is difficult to understand why the Portuguese, with all the fresh fish in the world, are so keen on *bacalhau.* Some Portuguese cookery books have at least 50 recipes for it. There is said to be a *bacalhau* recipe for every day of the year. Some people claim there are over 1,000 different ways of preparing *bacalhau,* but that seems a bit over the top.

We had not planned to include a *bacalhau* recipe in this book, but then we thought it a good idea to suggest the following as imaginative starters.

## SALTED COD CAKES *PASTEIS DE BACALHAU*

| | |
|---|---|
| *200 g bacalhau* | *2 eggs* |
| *1 garlic clove* | *1/2 onion* |
| *1 tsp ground paprika* | *2 cups flour* |
| *1 tsp baking powder* | *salt, pepper* |
| *oil to deep-fry* | |

Soak the *bacalhau* in water for 4 to 6 hours. Remove the skin and bones.

Purée the fish, garlic and onions in a blender or pass through a meat grinder.

Place into a bowl and add eggs and paprika. Season to taste with pepper and, if preferred, again with some salt.

Add a sufficient amount of flour mixed with baking powder to obtain a workable dough.

Heat oil in a saucepan.

Scoop teaspoon size portions from the dough and deep-fry in oil.

Serve on a base of green lettuce.

*Pataniscas de bacalhau,* are the Algarve's answer to fish-fingers.

## PATANISCAS DE BACALHAU

| | |
|---|---|
| *1 piece of bacalhau* | *1 tbsp oil* |
| *1 small onion* | *1 cup of flour* |
| *1 egg* | *milk* |
| *some lemon juice* | *parsley* |
| *salt, pepper* | *oil to deep-fry* |

As with the previous recipe, soak the *bacalhau* in water for 4 to 6 hours. Remove the skin and bones.

Cut into small fillet-like strips and keep them for 2 hours in a marinade of milk and lemon juice.

Prepare a batter using the flour, egg yolk, salt, pepper, chopped onion, parsley, oil and, if necessary, a small amount of water.

Dip each fish fillet into the batter and then deep-fry in oil.

Dry the fried fish on kitchen paper and sprinkle with salt according to taste.

Serve the *pataniscas* with a bean salad.

Winter time is hunting time. Anybody who can carry a gun, with or without permission, is walking with dogs across land, whether or not it is private or public property. Anything that moves is a target. In many cases the victims are young rabbits which therefore don't reach maturity.

Here is a rabbit recipe for which you will need a *cataplana* pan.

## RABBIT CATAPLANA *COELHO NA CATAPLANA*

| | |
|---|---|
| *1 rabbit, gutted and cleaned* | *1 glass strong, red wine* |
| *1 onion* | *2 garlic cloves* |
| *2 tbsp oil* | *2 tbsp lard* |
| *6 slices of finely cut bacon* | *parsley* |
| *salt, pepper* | |

Cut the rabbit into pieces, add salt and pepper.

Mix the red wine with chopped onion, chopped garlic, parsley and pepper.

Put the rabbit into this marinade. Cover and stand for 3 to 4 hours.

Heat the oil, lard and bacon in the *cataplana* pan.

Add the rabbit and close the *cataplana*. Stew for approximately 1 hour.

When the rabbit is done take it out. Bread slices can be fried in the remaining fat.

Serve the rabbit with olives and salad.

Rabbit is not the only game to be found and eaten in the Algarve. In the vicinity of Monchique there is wild boar and consequently roasted boar.

## Wild Boar with Chick Peas *JAVALI COM GRÃO*

| (Wild Boar) | 1 kg wild boar neck |
|:---:|:---:|
| 1 leek | 2 carrots |
| 2 onions | 2 garlic cloves |
| 2 cloves | 1 bay leaf |
| 1 sprig of thyme | 1 tbsp oil |
| 1/2 litre red wine | 1 cup water |
| salt | pepper |

Heat the oil in a roasting pan. Add the meat and fry on all

sides. Remove from the pan.

Add the chopped carrots, the leek and onion rings to the fat and brown.

Add water and red wine.

Then add the garlic, thyme, cloves and bay leaf. Season to taste with salt and pepper.

Place the meat on top of the vegetables and cover the pan.

Stew in a pre-heated oven of 160 - 180 degrees for 60 to possibly 90 minutes. Remove the meat from the pan.

Pass the vegetables and broth through a sieve and season the sauce to taste.

Cut the meat into slices and serve with sauce.

| (Chick Peas) | *150 g chick peas* |
|---|---|
| *1 onion* | *20 g butter* |
| *1 tbsp oil* | *2 tbsp chopped parsley* |
| *salt, pepper* | *1 litre water* |

Soak the chick peas in water overnight.

The next day cook them for approximately 1 hour. Take them out of the water and remove their skin. Return the peas to the stock.

Cook until they have reached a mushy consistency.

Season to taste with salt and pepper, blend butter and parsley into the peas.

Heat the oil in a saucepan. Cut the onion into rings and fry until brown. Pour over the mushy peas.

Turkeys have always been eaten in the Algarve at Christmas. One can buy turkey meat throughout the year, though outside of the Christmas period it is generally available only in portions rather than whole birds.

## LEG OF TURKEY *PERNA DE PERU*

| | |
|---|---|
| *4 turkey legs* | *1 bread roll* |
| *1 tbsp chopped onion* | *1 tbsp chopped parsley* |
| *1 tbsp chopped bacon* | *1 tbsp oil* |
| *1 egg* | *salt, pepper* |

Separate the meat from the bone by cutting the turkey leg at the top, the bottom and vertically. Remove the sinews.

Spice the legs with salt and pepper.

Cut the bread roll into small cubes and fry with the bacon.

In a separate bowl, mix the egg, parsley and onion. Season with salt and pepper.

Use this mixture to stuff the turkey legs. Fold them and close them with a tooth pick.

Heat the oil in a saucepan and fry the legs on all sides. Place them on a baking tray and bake them in the oven at a temperature of 150 degrees for approximately 30 to 40 minutes until they are tender.

Serve hot with vegetables or cold in cut slices.

Finally, a few sweets that go well with the Algarve winter.

## SWEET RICE PUDDING *ARROZ DOCE*

| | |
|---|---|
| 1 cup of rice | 2 egg yolk |
| 3 cups milk | 1/2 cup of sugar |
| 1 tsp ground lemon peel | 1 tsp vanilla sugar |
| 1 tbsp cinnamon | 1 tbsp sugar |

Put the rice into boiling water and after five minutes drain off the water.

Bring the milk with sugar and vanilla to the boil.

Add the rice and cover. Simmer until the rice is soft.

Break the egg yolk and mix with lemon peel. Stir this into the rice pudding.

Fill into small glass dishes and stand to cool.

Turn over and sprinkle with sugar and cinnamon.

## ORANGE ICE CREAM *GELADO DE LARANJA NA CASCA*

| | |
|---|---|
| 4 oranges | 500 g vanilla ice-cream |
| 1 small glass Cointreau | some ground orange peel |
| or | from an additional orange |
| Portuguese orange liqueur | |

Cut a third off the tops of four lovely big oranges. Keep aside as lids.

Carefully scoop out the flesh from the lids of the oranges and purée in a blender.

Mix the vanilla ice-cream with the orange purée and the ground orange peel. Season with the orange liqueur.

Pour the soft mixture back into the orange cases and close with the lids.

Place into the deep freeze compartment of the refrigerator and freeze.

Take out only just before serving. Wipe the moisture off the skin and serve in glass bowls.

## ORANGE ROLL *TORTA DE LARANJA*

| | |
|---|---|
| *6 eggs* | *250 g sugar* |
| *1 cup orange juice* | *2 tbsp ground orange peel* |
| *2 tbsp flour* | *1 tsp baking powder* |
| *2 tbsp orange marmalade* | *icing sugar to sprinkle* |

Whisk the eggs and sugar to a frothy consistency. Add the orange juice and peel.

Add the flour mixed with baking powder until the dough is smooth.

Cover a baking tray with grease-proof paper and spread the dough evenly at a height of a few centimetres.

Cover with grease-proof paper and dry, rather than bake, in a pre-heated oven of 150 - 180 degrees for 15 to 20 minutes.

Remove the paper. Spread marmalade across and fold into a roll while still warm.

Sprinkle with icing sugar.

When our baker friends in Guia, Isabel Conceição Correia and her husband, want to have a bit of fun with friends, they bake a very special bread.

## BAKER'S BREAD *PÃO DO PADEIRO*

| | |
|---|---|
| *500 g sugar* | *500 g ground almonds* |
| *20 egg yolks* | *1/2 cup lemon juice* |
| *1/2 litre water* | *some flour* |
| *2 cups fios de ovos* | *1 cup ovos moles* |
| *2 cups doce de chila* | *some ground chocolate* |

Cook sugar with water and lemon juice until it thickens to a caramel-like texture.

Add the peeled and ground almonds. Keep stirring until the dough has become thick.

Place into a bowl and knead the egg yolks into the dough. Stand to cool.

Take a round oven-proof dish and grease thoroughly, then roll the dough flat on a wooden board with flour.

Place half of the dough into the oven-proof dish and fill with *fios de ovos*, *ovos moles* and *doce de chila*. It doesn't matter in which order.

Cover with the remaining dough in such a way that the appearance is that of a round loaf.

If preferred, you can sprinkle ground chocolate on top. This will look as if the bread is slightly burnt.

Bake in a pre-heated oven of 150 - 180 degrees for approximately 30 to 45 minutes.

# A WINTER MENU
# FROM QUINTA DE SÃO BENTO
# IN MONCHIQUE

The view is breathtakingly beautiful and on a clear day one can see across the western Algarve all the way to the ocean.

Eating, drinking and living all happens under the same roof of a house owned by an aristocratic family. It is a life among antiques, every piece representing a snippet of Portugal's history.

You don't imagine anything like this exists, certainly not in the Algarve, but it does at Quinta de São Bento which is on the road leading up from Monchique to Fóia. It was built in 1948 as a holiday home and country residence for the Infanta Dona Filipa de Bragança. It still belongs to the Bragança family.

The Bragança dynasty ruled Portugal - and for some time Brazil too - from 1640 to 1853 and then, with a few interruptions, until 1910. If Portugal had a king today, he would be the current Duke of Bragança, Dom Duarte, but there is little public interest in a restoration of the monarchy.

There are three gastronomic enterprises at the Quinta and it is possible to stay overnight. There are five rooms and an apartment. Each is furnished individually and to the highest standard with precious antiques.

There is the Jardim dos Castanheiros, a garden restaurant with 160 seats; the Infanta Dona Filipa restaurant which seats 42; and a bar called Tertulia.

Marieta Monteiro is the manager. She was born in Monchique, but this is not the only reason why she has such a good rapport with the Algarve and the hills. She is a historian and has studied the customs and traditions of the region. That is why all the rooms are so beautifully decorated and the smallest detail lovingly attended to. This is noticeable right from the start of any meal here.

When you sit down at a table in Quinta de São Bento you receive in addition to garlic bread and butter, small baskets and cloth bags containing regional specialities. There are almonds and figs, *chouriço*, goat's cheese made by a lady in Santa Clara, and ham from Monchique. And there are pickled carrots, *conserva de cenouras*, the first recipe in the winter menu arranged for us by Marieta Monteiro.

## PICKLED CARROTS *CONSERVA DE CENOURAS*

| | |
|---|---|
| 250 g carrots | 1 small bay leaf |
| 1/2 tsp caraway seeds | 2 onions, cut into rings |
| 3 tbsp olive oil | 1 cup of black olives |
| 1 tbsp chopped parsley | 1 pinch of sweet |
| 1 tbsp vinegar | ground paprika |
| salt | |

Clean the carrots and cut into slices approximately 1 cm thick. Cook with bay leaf and caraway seeds in a little water. They must not become too soft. Remove from the liquid.

Brown the onion rings in olive oil, then pour into a bowl.

Add the carrots and olives and mix carefully.

Blend the vinegar with salt, paprika and parsley and pour over the carrots. Stand to cool for a few hours before serving.

Marieta Monteiro has collected a multitude of cooking instructions, some of them very old. The recipe for our second course originates in the 16th century. It is a substantial soup and just the right thing for the winter.

## CHICKEN SOUP *GALINHA ENSOPADA*

| | |
|---|---|
| 1/2 chicken | 4 eggs |

| | |
|---|---|
| *2 egg yolks* | *1 tbsp parsley* |
| *1 tbsp coriander* | *1 tbsp celery green* |
| *2 tbsp olive oil* | *1 small chopped onion* |
| *1 1/2 litre water* | *salt, pepper,* |
| *cinnamon* | *some stale bread* |

Cook the chicken until soft in 1 1/2 litres of salted water with the onion, oil and half of the herbs.

Pass the broth through a sieve.

Remove skin and bones from the chicken and tear the meat into very thin strips.

Pour part of the broth into a new pot and bring to the boil. Slip the 4 eggs whole into the broth, poach, scoop them and set aside.

Pass the 2 egg yolks through a fine sieve, mix with a little cold water and pour into the broth.

Season to taste with salt and pepper.

Place 5 small and very thinly cut slices of stale bread into the base of each soup bowl in a circular pattern.

Distribute the chicken meat over them and sprinkle with herbs.

Place a poached egg in the centre and top up with hot chicken broth. In the end, season with a touch of cinnamon.


The next course will be meat - kid - prepared à la maison. It is a speciality of the Quinta's kitchen team. By the way, the kitchen team is entirely female, one more indication that women are by far the better cooks in the region, although as mentioned elsewhere in this book, there are some exceptions.

## KID QUINTA SÃO BENTO-STYLE *CABRITO À QUINTA SÃO BENTO*

| | |
|---|---|
| 1 1/2 kg kid meat (for example the legs) | 1 onion |
| 1 tsp rose paprika | 3 garlic cloves |
| 2 tbsp chopped parsley | 1 bay leaf |
| 1 1/2 litre water | 1/4 litre white wine |
| | 1 tsp massa de pimentos |

| | |
|---|---|
| (for the sauce) | 1 tbsp butter |
| 2 tbsp olive oil | 2 tbsp oil |
| 1 tsp massa de pimento | three chopped garlic cloves |
| 125 ml white wine | salt, pepper |

| | |
|---|---|
| (Side-dishes) | 2 carrots |
| 12 prunes | shallots |
| champignons | 500 g potatoes |
| oil to fry | |

Cook the *massa de pimentos*, onion, bay leaf, parsley, garlic and paprika with wine, salt and water into a broth.

Put the kid meat into the broth and continue to cook until done.

Remove the bones from the meat and split into portions.

Prepare the sauce by cooking butter, oil, *massa de pimentos*, salt and crushed garlic with wine on a low heat for approximately five minutes.

For the side-dish cut the potatoes into large cubes and briefly fry in oil. Do not allow to become too soft.

Place the meat into a large oven-proof dish and pour the sauce over it.

Cut the carrots into slices, clean and halve the champignons.

Remove stones from the prunes. Place prunes and shallots decoratively across the meat. Cover with potatoes.

Use only as much of the broth as is needed to cover the dish.

Bake in a pre-heated oven at a temperature of 250 degrees for approximately 30 minutes.

As an alternative to kid use lamb.


For dessert there is *Leite creme* made according to a very traditional recipe. Formerly, when milk was much richer, this dessert could be made without the addition of cream or corn-flour. It is now possible to buy *leite creme* as a ready-made mix, but it is unlikely to compare with what you will be served at Quinta de São Bento.

# EGG CUSTARD *LEITE CREME*

| | |
|---|---|
| *1/2 litre milk* | *1/4 litre double cream* |
| *1 cup sugar* | *1 tbsp cornflour* |
| *some milk* | *1 tbsp ground lemon peel* |
| *6 egg yolk* | *1/2 cup milk* |
| *sugar to sprinkle* | |

Bring the milk, cream and sugar to the boil. Stir continuously.

Mix the cornflour with some cold milk and add to the hot liquid.

Whisk the egg to a frothy consistency, add some milk and the lemon peel. Fold into the hot liquid.

Measure into plates and stand to cool.

Sprinkle with sugar.

Take a kitchen branding iron and create designs on the cream. If you don't have such a tool, you can use a heated potato masher.

# FESTIVE DAYS

Once the days become shorter and most tourists have left the Algarve, the time has come for the Algarvians to celebrate. These days of celebration are festive family days and they start in November.

On All Saints Day, *Dia de Todos os Santos,* candles are lit on cemeteries to commemorate the dead. On this day too, godparents bake cake for their godchildren who come visiting. Here's the recipe for the cake.

# PÃO - DE - LÓ

| (for the cake) | 12 eggs |
|---|---|
| 400 g sugar | 150 g flour |
| 100 g cornflour | 200 g ground almonds |

(for filling) either

| 2 cups ovos moles, | or 2 cups doce de chila |
|---|---|
| 2 cups fios de ovos | or 400 g marzipan |
| or 2 cups orange marmalade | or 200 g cooking chocolate |
| 1 tbsp butter | 1/2 litre milk |
| 1 cup sugar | 1 tbsp cornflour |

Separate the eggs. Whisk the sugar and egg yolk into a frothy consistency.

Gradually add the flour and cornflour.

(Should you want to make *pão-de-ló de amêndoas,* add the ground almonds at this point).

Whisk the egg white until very stiff and carefully fold into the mixture.

Spread the dough onto a well-greased baking tray and place in a cold oven.

Bake at a temperature of 80 - 100 degrees for 10 to 20 minutes.

Place on a cooking grid and cut in half.

Cover one half with one of the above fillings and position

the other half on top. Lightly press together.

If you use an *ovos moles* filling, garnish with *fios de ovos*. Otherwise sprinkle with icing sugar.

For the chocolate filling, melt the chocolate in a small saucepan on a very low heat.

Stir butter and sugar into it. Mix cornflour with some milk and fold into the liquid chocolate. Bring to the boil just once.

While still warm, spread this mixture on to the dough.

All Saints Day is the day for eating stuffed figs as a traditional sweet.

On St. Martin's Day, people say: "*Vai à adega e prova o vinho!*" (Let's go to the cellar and taste the wine!) The new wine is sampled and so is the *água pé*. As appetizers, people will eat little snacks such as pieces of sausage, bread and olives and above all, salted and roasted chestnuts.

Advent is heralded with the sale of *Bolo rei* from the end of November until the middle of January. *Bolo rei* takes its name from the biblical three kings and symbolizes one of the presents they gave to the child Jesus. In all Portuguese provinces, including the Algarve, *Bolo rei* is as much part of Christmas as pudding and mince pies are with us.

## KING'S CAKE *BOLO REI*

| *20 g yeast* | *some milk* |

| | |
|---|---|
| 500 g flour | 100 g butter |
| 150 g sugar | 3 eggs |
| 100 g ground walnuts | 100 g raisins |
| 1 tbsp lemon juice | 3 tbsp orange juice |
| 1/2 glass port wine | 1/2 cup candied orange peel |
| 1/2 cup candied lemon peel | some salt |
| some candied fruit to garnish | 1 egg yolk to brush |

Prepare the yeast in warm milk and some flour. Stand for 10 minutes.

Soak the raisins in port wine. Cut the candied orange and lemon peel into small pieces and turn in flour.

Place the remainder of the flour into a bowl and make an indentation in the centre. Fill it with the yeast.

Add butter, sugar, eggs, a pinch of salt and knead into a dough. Then add the nuts, raisins, orange and lemon peel, juice and wine. Work your hands repeatedly through the dough.

Cover the dough with a piece of cloth and stand at a warm spot. Allow to rise until it has reached twice its size.

Again knead some flour into the dough and split into three portions to form ropes.

Take a round baking ring and grease well. Plait the cords and place into the baking ring. Stand for another 30 minutes.

Cover with candied fruits and brush egg yolk over the dough. The *Bolo rei* should look like a richly ornamented crown.

There is an old tradition connected to *Bolo rei*. One usually bakes a broad bean and a small present into the cake. Whoever finds the present is, of course, allowed to keep it - it will bring luck. Whoever finds the bean is committed to bake everyone present at the table a second *Bolo rei*. (Other sources say the finder must bake next year's *Bolo rei*).

Opinions vary as to precisely what time *Bolo rei* is supposed to be eaten. Let's just stick to Christmas.

At Christmas the entire family will get together to share one sumptuous meal after another. This involves non-stop activity in the kitchen and all cooking and baking is traditionally done by the women. Ah, traditions!

At Christmas practically everyone in the Algarve, as well as in most other Portuguese households, eats *bacalhau* for the main course. The starter will be a soup and for dessert there will be cheese, sweets and fruit.

On one of the festive days there will certainly be *Perú recheado*, turkey stuffed with potatoes or meat, or there will be suckling pig on the table.

## SUCKLING PIG *LEITÃO*

| | |
|---|---|
| *1 kg of suckling pig, the neck or rack* | *1 tbsp oil* |
| *1 tbsp water* | *1 tsp honey (preferably rosemary honey)* |
| *1 tbsp water* | *1 sprig of thyme* |
| *salt, pepper* | |

Rub salt and pepper into the pork and stand for a while.

Heat the oil in a saucepan and fry the meat on all sides. Add the thyme and roast in a pre-heated oven of 180 degrees for 40 to 50 minutes.

Mix the water with the honey and spread over the meat. Keep for another 10 minutes in the oven to obtain a nice crust.

As a dessert, *filhós* have a distinct tradition. They are accompanied by *aguardente*. But there are other desserts. *Pudim flan* is one of the most popular in the Algarve even though it probably originated elsewhere. The best way to make it is by using little pastry moulds.

## CRÊME CARAMEL *PUDIM FLAN*

| 1 cup sugar | 3 eggs |
|---|---|
| 1 vanilla pod | 1/4 litre milk |

Whisk one tablespoon of sugar and the eggs to a frothy consistency. On a very low heat, gently stir this into luke warm milk.

Cut the vanilla pod open and scrape out the inside. Add this to the cream.

In a separate pot, melt the remaining sugar and stir continuously until brown.

Pour the caramel into four small pastry moulds and top up

with the egg mixture. Place a bowl with hot water and cook very carefully for 30 minutes.

Remember not to allow the water to boil and splash into the moulds. Remove the moulds and stand to cool.

Just before turning them out, dip them briefly into hot water.

In bygone days, only the very best pieces of the pig killed in November were served at table at Christmas. These were the ribs, the neck and cutlets. They were served along with sausages, mussels and other seafood. As a side dish, *Fatias com carne* (fried bread slices) were served.

## FATIAS COM CARNE

| | |
|---|---|
| *4 slices of stale bread* | *4 tbsp milk* |
| *1 tbsp olive oil* | *1 egg* |
| *salt, pepper* | *fat to fry* |

Soak the stale bread slices in milk and sprinkle some olive oil on top.

Mix the egg with salt and pepper and place bread slices into it; turn. Fry the slices in hot fat.

Just before frying, the bread slices can be sprinkled with crushed garlic, according to taste.

The Algarvians like to see the New Year in with friends and

relations in hotels and restaurants rather than at home.

But on Epiphany, the 12th night of Christmas, the entire family will get together again. *Bolo rei* and pomegranates are eaten. According to folklore, "if you haven't eaten pomegranates by the 6th of January, you won't have any money throughout the year"

The next big festival is *Carnaval*, a fun time, celebrated all over the Algarve but particularly in Loulé. Shrove Tuesday is the most celebrated of all carnival days. There is a big procession and lots to drink.

At meal times there will be chicken dishes such as *Galo entrudo, Cabidela* or *Frango piri-piri.*

*Cabidela* is a meal which may not be quite to your taste, but here is a brief description of how it is prepared. Brown onion, garlic and parsley in a saucepan. Cut a chicken into portions, sprinkle with salt and pepper and add to the pot. Top up with chicken stock. You can also add chicken blood (supplied with supermarket chickens), but you will have to add vinegar to stop it from coagulating. Cook the chicken in this liquid until tender.

For dessert there will certainly be *nuvens.*

## CLOUD PUFFS *NUVENS*

| | |
|---|---|
| *1/2 litre milk* | *1 cup sugar* |
| *6 eggs* | *1 tbsp ground lemon peel* |
| *1 tsp cinnamon* | |

Bring the sugar, lemon peel and milk to the boil. Separate the eggs.

Whisk the egg white until very stiff.

With a teaspoon, drop small portions of egg white into the hot milk. Scoop out after approximately one minute.

Remove the milk from the heat and whisk the egg yolk into the liquid to a creamy consistency.

Fill dessert plates, first with egg cream then place a few cloud puffs on top and sprinkle with cinnamon.

*Carnaval*, when the evil spirits are supposed to be banished, brings us back to where we started: almond blossom and springtime once again......

*Bom apetite!*

# RECIPE INDEX